CHANGE YOUR
HABITS
CHANGE YOUR
LIFE

THOMAS C. CORLEY

EMBASSY BOOKS
www.embassybooks.in

CHANGE YOUR HABITS CHANGE YOUR LIFE
by Thomas C. Corley

This edition first published in 2019

Published in India by:
Embassy Book Distributors
120, Great Western Building,
Maharashtra Chamber of Commerce Lane,
Fort, Mumbai - 400 023.
Tel : (91-22) 22819546 / 22818567.
Email : info@embassybooks.in
Website : www.embassybooks.in

Distribution Centres:
Mumbai, Bangalore, Kolkata, Chennai,
Hyderabad, New Delhi, Pune

ISBN: 978-93-88247-13-9

Page layout and design: PSV Kumarasamy

Printed : SAP Print Solutions Pvt. Ltd., Mumbai

Contents

ACKNOWLEDGEMENTS

Nothing worthwhile ever gets accomplished without a team of people behind you. This entire Rich Habits journey I've been on these past eleven years has brought me close to some amazing people who I like to think are part of my team. These amazing individuals have helped to shine a light on my Rich Habits research. They literally pulled me out of a cave and gave me a microphone.

Darren Hardy, publisher of SUCCESS Magazine, was kind enough to interview me for the November 2014 edition of SUCCESS Magazine and now nearly 300,000 individuals know who I am and what my Rich Habits are all about. Thank you so much Darren.

Libby Kane of Business Insider has become one of my favorite cheerleaders. Libby's given me the opportunity to share my Rich Habits research with millions of Business Insider readers. I very much appreciate Libby for opening the door and inviting me in to Business Insider as a contributor. Thank you Libby for your incredible support.

Hillcrest Media, my publisher, does such an amazing job

editing and producing my books and they've done it again with this latest book. I appreciate each and every one of the dedicated staff at Hillcrest whose passion for what they do has transformed my books into both bestsellers and award-winning books. Thank you Hillcrest for all you do.

I'd also like to thank Paula Andrea whose feedback helped me refine and improve my book. Paula devoted an enormous amount of time in identifying many ways to improve my book, in particular the section on Financial Success. Thank you Paula.

INTRODUCTION

No matter what you may believe, you have the ability to change the circumstances of your life. You can go from average to success. From mediocrity to wealth. You are not defined by your past or current circumstances. Circumstances can be changed. But in order to change your circumstances you need three things:

1. Daily Growth (in skills and knowledge).

2. Focus.

3. Persistence.

By using the habit change strategies in this book, you will acquire these three characteristics of success. Habits, by their very definition, are persistent routines. When you adopt good habits, they will help you grow in skill and knowledge. Good daily habits enable you to focus every day on pursuing success. Each good habit you add to your life has a cumulative effect. They are like an investment in your individual success. The key is to get your personal Habit Seesaw tipping in the right direction, with your Rich Habits outweighing your Poor Habits. Getting control of your habits is empowering. It gives you a sense of control over your life. According to the latest research on happiness, having a feeling of control over your life is one of the most significant drivers in creating happiness. Your new habits will not only put you on the path to success, they will also put you on the path to happiness. Your life will never be the same.

PART I
UNDERSTANDING
HABITS

THE PURPOSE OF HABITS

Habits have a purpose. They save the brain from work and help conserve brain fuel. Habits allow each of us to perform tasks without thinking. Habits are really three things: they are unconscious behaviors, unconscious thinking and unconscious decisions we make. Habits are governed by a golf ball sized area of the brain called the basal ganglia. The basal ganglia resides deep within the brain, in an area known as the limbic system. It is the unconscious command and control center for habits. When the basal ganglia decides that a habit needs to go to work, it instructs the brain to fire up specific brain cells and once fired, we find ourselves unconsciously engaging in some behavior, thinking or decision-making. I'll get into this in a more detail in the pages that follow.

Unless we force ourselves to become aware of our habits, we will never be able to change our habitual actions, habitual thinking or habitual behavior. It slips right below the radar of our consciousness. Habits are, quite simply, an amazing invention.

Studies show that many of our habits come from our

parents, our first important role models. According to these studies, parents have the most influence over the habits we develop in our childhood and most of these habits we carry with us into our adult years. Parents infect kids with their habits. Some of this parental habit mimicking is neurological. Our brains have something called mirror neurons. The purpose of mirror neurons is to enable babies and children to mimic the behaviors and emotions of their parents. They are an ancient relic of prehistoric human evolution, whose primary purpose for existing is to aid in survival. Some of this parental mimicking is also environmental. Kids are always tuned in and watching the behaviors of their parents. And lastly, some of it is forced upon kids; parents, mandating and encouraging certain behaviors. A study of 50,000 American families by Dr. Pressman, Director of Research for the New England Center for Pediatric Psychology out of Brown University (The American Journal of Family Therapy, published in 2014) found that habits in children are unlikely to vary much after the age of 9.

Only when kids become adults, are they able to break free from the habits forged during their early lives. Their new habits develop from new environments, career mentors, life-long self-education or from the school of hard knocks.

In another study on habits, this one conducted by Duke University in 2006, it was determined that an average of 40% of all daily human activities are habits. Habits include both physical and mental behavior. These daily habits unconsciously control our lives. Our daily habits, as boring as they may be, are the secret to success, failure or mediocrity. Our habitual behaviors, both physical and mental, and the choices we make, are the cause of wealth and poverty. Those who learn good daily habits from their parents, a mentor or through the school of hard knocks, excel in life. Their lives are outstanding. They rule the world. They command respect, make most of the money in this world, and control the lives of millions who do not have good daily habits. Our daily habits are the reason we live in a beach house or a slum. They are the reason we make millions of dollars a year or eke out a living, forced to live paycheck to paycheck. Our daily habits are the reason we are happy or unhappy. Our daily habits are the reason our children go to the best colleges or struggle to graduate from high school. The blueprint of our life and the lives of our children are determined by daily habits. That's how important habits are. If you want to change your life you must change your daily habits.

HABITS AND YOUR BRAIN

Habits are nothing more than specific brain cells that talk to one another frequently. Frequency is the key. When the brain notices certain brain cells constantly chatting with one another, the brain puts a 'habit" label on them. These "habit" brain cells are like little computers that are all linked, like computers are linked in a computer network, to another group of brain cells deep inside the brain called the basal ganglia. The basal ganglia is that golf ball size mass of brain cells I mentioned a few pages ago. It has many purposes, one of which is controlling habits. Think of the basal ganglia as the central computer for habits. One of its jobs is to oversee habits. When it sees an opportunity, the basal ganglia does one of two things:

1. Labels certain brain cells as "habits" and
2. Instructs those brain cells when to begin a habit

When the basal ganglia sees an opportunity to start a habit, it sends a signal to the front part of our brain that it's time to engage in a habit. The moment the front part of the brain receives this signal, it sends a command and those "habit" brain cells then tell us to engage is some habitual behavior.

Why does the brain do this? Why are habits so important to the brain? Habits save the brain from work, which means the brain uses less energy, less fuel. When the brain engages in a habit, it requires almost no work. It's an unconscious act. This is important because thinking and other conscious acts consume a great deal of glucose and oxygen. Glucose is the fuel supply to every cell in the human body, including the brain. All the food we consume is eventually converted into glucose, or stored for later use in our fat or muscles. Glucose passes through each cell and once inside the cell, it is violently ripped apart and converted to use as fuel. Converting glucose to cell fuel requires oxygen. Each day our little 3 1/2 pound brains consume 20% of the entire body's supply of glucose and oxygen. Unlike the rest of the body, which can store glucose in fat and muscle, the brain can't store glucose. The brain has no readily available supply of fuel to use when it needs it. For this reason, glucose is considered a precious commodity to the brain. Habits reduce the brain's need for this precious brain fuel.

With respect to the brain, habits are an investment. In the beginning of the formation of any habit, the brain invests precious brain fuel in the creation of a habit. This habits creation process is like building a house. A lot of work goes into constructing the house, but once the house is built, the construction work ends. It's the same thing with habits. Once the habit is formed, there's very little work required by the brain in maintaining or engaging in a habit. It's very efficient. And the brain likes efficient.

Habits require less brain fuel. For these two reasons, efficiency and fuel conservation, the brain naturally likes habits, encourages habits and fights us when we abandon or try to change an existing habit. That is why habit change is so hard - our own brain goes to war with us, each time we try to change a habit.

According to a famous study by University College of London, performed on 96 people, the habit formation process took anywhere from 18 to 254 days, with the average habit taking 66 days to form. The study also found that the more complex the behavior, such as swinging a golf club, the more time it took for a habit to form. Less complex habits, such as teaching children to brush their teeth every day, could be formed in a matter of days. This study made clear that habits come in many shapes, sizes and shades. Each with its own unique level of complexity and influence over our daily lives. The adoption of some habits affects our lives more than others. One powerful habit, in other words, can offset three or more less powerful habits, in terms of the consequences they have on our lives. Smoking cigarettes, for instance, is a bad habit that can negatively offset the benefits of daily exercise and good nutrition.

But who wants to wait as long as 254 days for a new habit to stick? I don't. You're looking at 254 days of hell, quite frankly. This is why New Year's resolutions only last a few weeks. The brain eventually forces you back into your old habits. There's a much easier way to change your habits. There are ways we can fool the brain into enthusiastically embracing habit change. But unless you know how to fool the brain into adding or removing a habit, you're going to lose the war and habit change will be impossible.

In this book I will share with you the unique strategies I uncovered in my research that will allow you to fool the brain into changing your habits. Instead of fighting you on habit change, these strategies will actually seduce the brain into wanting to change a habit. When your brain becomes a partner with you in changing your habits, habit change occurs immediately, which means your life begins to change immediately. Money problems, relationship struggles, work issues, poor health and many other parts of your life that are just not going well at all, will immediately begin to change for the better once you change your habits.

HABITS CAN CHANGE YOUR DNA

Did you know that your daily habits can turn genes on or off? It's known as gene expression or epigenetics. Gene expression is a process in which certain genes are turned on or off during one's lifetime. The human body contains approximately 100 trillion cells. Within each cell is the nucleus. Inside every nucleus of every cell are our genes. Experts estimate that the average human has over 20,000 genes. Some of these genes came from our mothers and some from our fathers.

Believe it or not, your daily habits can turn genes on or off. Bad habits can turn off good genes and turn on bad genes. This could mean opening the door to cancer, diabetes, various addictions, brain damage, heart disease, etc. Bad habits can create long-term stress in the form of financial problems, job loss, health issues, etc. Long-term stress increases the production of cortisol, a stress hormone. Like a domino effect, cortisol switches on a series of bad genes that can lead to heart disease, cancer and immunological disorders.

Some of the bad habits that turn bad genes on include:

- Excessive alcohol consumption.

- Drug use.

- Not eating healthy or eating too much junk food can change your DNA.

- Lack of daily aerobic exercise.

- Consuming too much sugar.

- Not exercising our brains by reading or learning new skills.

- Negative emotions and negative thinking.

Conversely, good habits can turn bad genes off and turn good genes on. The byproduct of good habits is reduced stress resulting from financial independence, happiness, good health, etc. Some of these good habits include:

- Daily reading or learning new skills, which can turn on genes that increase your IQ.

- Daily aerobic exercise, which can turn on genes that prevent heart disease, asthma and other immunological disorder.

- Meditation, which can turn off bad genes that contribute to the onset of various types of diseases and turn on good genes that prevent such diseases.

- Positive thinking and positive emotions alter the brain's chemistry which increases or decreases gene expression.

Habits are not harmless. They can alter your DNA by changing your genome. This is important but not just for you. When you change your DNA you can pass along this altered DNA to your children, for better or for worse.

HABIT FORMATION

Thanks to the amazing research of Charles Duhigg, author of The Power of Habit, we have a much better understanding of the process that drive habits: the cue, the routine and the reward. The cue represents a familiar environmental point of reference that sends a message to the basal ganglia that it is time to engage in a habit. This is one of the reasons why environmental changes can disrupt habits, which we'll get into a little later. Once we are exposed to this environmental trigger, the basal ganglia takes over and directs us to engage in the routine. At the end of the routine is a reward waiting for us. Example: You're driving in the car with your kids and one of them screams out, "McDonald's. I want to go to McDonald's." Your child just noticed the golden arches and immediately began thinking about the delicious chicken McNuggets inside the building behind the golden arches. So you turn right at the golden arches (the cue), pull into McDonald's (the routine), and your kids gorge themselves with McNuggets (the reward).

This process repeats itself with every habit. Instead of golden arches, it might be a pot of coffee (time for the coffee habit) or your Friday routine after work (time for the beer or wine habit), or turning on your computer (time for the check email habit). Every habit has a cue, a routine and a reward.

Habits are formed over many years of repetitive behavior and thinking. Habits are the by-product of common brain cells repeatedly talking with one another. Brain experts call this brain cell chatter a synapse. The more frequent the brain cells talk with one another the stronger the synapse becomes. Brain cells that talk to each other, in a sense marry one another. They are often stuck with each other for life. Sometimes, when certain brain cells talk to each other enough, the basal ganglia, the command and control center for habits in the brain, will label them as habits. It does this in order to save the brain from work, which also saves the brain from using fuel. Once the basal ganglia labels brain cells as habits, those brain cells remain habits forever. They never get unlabeled. This means you will be stuck with your habits forever unless you know the secrets to habit change. There are unique strategies that we'll cover in this book that will help you fool the brain into getting rid of habits that are holding you back in life and adding habits that will launch you into another dimension - into the top 5%. Those rare individuals who are happy and successful in life.

WHERE DO YOUR HABITS COME FROM?

Where did you pick up most of your habits in life? I'll bet you never gave it much thought. Your habits did not just manifest out of thin air. They came from some source. Each source, good or bad, inspired you to adopt certain habits. The habits we adopt in life primarily come through associations we make in life, our education, our experiences and our environment. Below is a list of the sources of our habits in their order of influence:

- Parents

- Mentors

- Informal Education – Reading Books

- The School of Hard Knocks – Learning From Mistakes and Failures

- Formal Education

- Your Culture

- Your Environment

- Siblings

- Spouse or Significant Other

- Friends

- Schoolmates

- Fellow Workers

- Grandparents

- In-Laws (Spouse or Significant Other's Family)

- Teammates

- Public Figures - Celebrities, Professional Athletes and Famous People

I'd like to drill a little deeper into the most influential sources for the habits we pick up in life.

Parents

By far the fountain of most good or bad habits we pick up in life is our parents. Many adult habits are forged in childhood. Kids watch what their parents do and then emulate them, good or bad. The self-made millionaires and poor people in my study picked up specific good or bad habits from their parents that unknowingly set them on the path to wealth or poverty in their adult lives. According to my data, 75% of the self-made millionaires in my Rich Habits Study learned good success habits from their parents. A recent study by Brown University, in which nearly 50,000 families were surveyed, concluded that habits in children are unlikely to vary after age nine (*https://www.psychologytoday.com/ blog/school-thought/201502/study-finds-habits-in-children- take-root-age-9*). Since kids are going to pick up most of their adult habits from their parents, parents can become success mentors to their kids; teaching them good habits that will help them succeed in life. Taking a look at any self-made millionaire in my study you find at least one parent who taught them success habits. Let's take a look at a few:

- *Warren Buffet* - Warren Buffet's father was a stock broker. It's no accident that Buffet became the world's best known value investor. He was mentored by his dad.

- *The Kennedy's* - Joseph Kennedy was a very successful politician who mentored sons JFK, Bobby Kennedy and Teddy Kennedy.

- *Ken Griffey, Jr.* - Ken Griffey Jr., arguably the most talented baseball player ever, was mentored by his professional baseball player-dad, Ken Griffey (NY Yankees).

- *Bill Belichick* - Bill Belichick's father was a football coach for Navy for 33 years. At age three Bill could be found on the knee of his father watching film of Navy football players.

The stories of parents who raised successful, millionaire children all have one thing in common: good habits. It's not an accident that their children excelled in life. They were taught by one or more parents certain success habits that elevated them above the competition as adults. Parents are often the only shot most have at having a mentor in life, which is the next source of habits we will discuss.

Mentors

The second greatest source of your habits comes from mentors. According to my data, 24% of the self-made millionaires in my study adopted habits taught to them by career mentors. Of these 24%, a whopping 93% said that the habits they learned from their career-mentors were responsible for almost all of the wealth they accumulated in life. The average net liquid wealth of the 233 millionaires in my study was $4.3 million. Finding a career mentor, therefore, is like someone depositing millions of dollars into your bank account.

Below is a list of some famously successful people who had a mentor in life:

- *Oprah Winfrey* - mentored by Mrs. Duncan (4th grade teacher).

- *General Colin Powell* - mentored by his father Luther Powell.

- *Dr. Martin Luther King* - mentored by Dr. Benjamin E. Mays.

- *Henry David Thoreau* - mentored by Ralph Waldo Emerson.

- *Senator John McCain* - mentored by William Ravenel (high school teacher/coach).

- Walter Cronkite - mentored by Fred Birney (high school journalism teacher).

- *Gloria Estefan* - mentored by her grandmother Consuelo Garcia.

- Helen Keller - mentored by Anne Sullivan.

- Bob Dylan - mentored by Woody Guthrie.

- Quincy Jones - mentored by Ray Charles.

- *Martin Sheen* - mentored by Rev. Alfred Drapp.

- *Denzel Washington* - mentored by Sidney Poitier.

- *Rosa Parks* - mentored by Alice L. White (headmistress).

- *Tom Brokaw* - mentored by Frances Morrow (elementary school teacher).

- *Mitch Albom* - mentored by Morrie Schwartz (Tuesdays with Morrie).

- *Larry King* - mentored by Edward Bennett Williams.

- *Tim Russert* - mentored by Sister Mary Lucille.

- *Jack Canfield* - mentored by C. Clement Stone, Mark Victor Hansen, Janet Switzer, John Gray, Bob Proctor, Jim Rohn and John Maxwell.

Case Study on Mentoring - Jamie Dimon

Jamie Dimon is one of the most successful, respected bankers in the world. Dimon was mentored by the legendary broker/banker Sandy Weill. The Weill-Dimon team was legendary for how intensely they worked together and how many mega-deals they collaborated on. It was a far cry from the typical employer/employee pairing. In 1983, Weill, then at American Express, hired a young, eager Dimon (whose stockbroker father had worked for Weill) when he was just 26 and fresh out of Harvard Business School. Weill left American Express two years later, and Dimon followed his mentor. The two of them worked side-by-side for many months, studying potential opportunities. Eventually, they found one they liked called Commercial Credit, a struggling lender in Baltimore, The duo took it Commercial Credit public, using it as a base with which to build their empire. What followed was a string of mergers culminating in the1998 merger of Weill's and Dimon's companies, with financial powerhouse, Citibank. Dimon benefited enormously from this much older and very wise mentor, eventually becoming the CEO of JP Morgan, one of the most powerful financial institutions in the world. When you find a career mentor in life, it puts you on the fast track of success.

Informal Education – Reading Books

Many successful people attribute their success in life to self-help, success authors such as Dale Carnegie, Earl Nightingale, Og Mandino or Jack Canfield. Co-founder of Microsoft and tech icon Bill Gates has made no secret of his passion for books. Gates loves to read, and loves to share what he's reading with others through the Gates

Notes Bookshelf, full of book reviews, books he's read, and books he wants to share with the world. Beyond recommendations, the Bill & Melinda Gates Foundation has made it a mission to bring and keep more useful technology in U.S. libraries and libraries around the world. On a more personal level, the Gates home stands as a testament to his love of reading, with a 2,100 square foot private library, complete with a domed reading room, and a Leonardo da Vinci notebook valued at nearly $31 million.

The School of Hard Knocks

Fifty one percent of the self-made millionaires in my Rich Habits Study were business owners. Twenty seven percent of these millionaires failed at least once in business. But like phoenix's they rose from the ashes of their failures and mistakes, poorer, but much wiser. The school of hard knocks is perhaps the hardest way to pick up good habits. When you run or start a business you will make many mistakes. When you make a mistake in business, it costs you time and money. Because it costs you time and money, the lessons stick. You either figure out what to do and what not to do, or you go under. You become your own mentor through the school of hard knocks. The most successful businesses in the world are built on top of a mountain of mistakes. The more successful you are as a business owner, very likely, the more mistakes you made along the way.

WHAT TRIGGERS A HABIT?

Every habit begins with a trigger. Triggers set in motion every habit you have. That basal ganglia we talked about early, is the command and control center for habits. It is always hunting for triggers in our environment in order to set a habit in motion. As mentioned previously, habits enable the brain to work less. Less work translates into less fuel usage. The basal ganglia, in a sense, is also the brain's fuel efficiency manager, using habits as its main energy savings device. Once a habit is triggered, you unconsciously engage in the habit. There are 6 primary habit triggers that set most habits in motion:

1. ***Visual Triggers*** - Visual Triggers are like external neon-colored billboards that scream at you to engage in a habit. The McDonald's arches are an example of a powerful Visual Trigger. Beer commercials are another example. Attractive women eating Doritos is yet another.

2. ***Auditory (Hearing) Triggers*** - Hearing something can set in motion a habit. When the alarm clock goes off, that's a trigger to wake up and start our day. When we hear an email alert, that's a trigger to

check our email. When we hear our baby crying, we know it's time for a diaper change or feeding.

3. *Time of Day Triggers* - We all have habits that we engage in during the morning, afternoon and evening. Waking up in the morning is a trigger that sets in motion all sorts of habits: drinking coffee, exercise, brushing your teeth, taking a shower, reading, meditating, going to the bathroom, etc. Afternoon Triggers set off your afternoon habits: eating lunch, gossiping, reading, surfing the Internet, making personal phone calls, networking, meetings with other people, etc. Nighttime prompts you to engage in nighttime habits: eating dinner, a glass of wine, watching T.V., reading, making personal phone calls, exercise, engaging in a hobby or extracurricular activity, gardening, going to a bar, etc.

4. *Stress Triggers* - Stress can force you to engage in a habit. Stress overwhelms the brain, consuming far too much fuel. To compensate, the basal ganglia is put to work, prodding you to find a habit to engage in in order to conserve brain fuel.

5. *Association Triggers* - People who you associate with are habit triggers. One friend can be a trigger for hitting the bars, another for exercising, another for gambling, yet another for golfing, fishing, tennis, etc. Who you associate with are habit triggers. This is why you should avoid individuals with bad habits. They drag you down by triggering bad habits.

6. ***Beliefs and Emotions*** – Our beliefs and emotions trigger habits. Negative beliefs and emotions trigger bad habits and positive beliefs and emotions trigger good habits. If you want to eliminate a bad habit, you need to eliminate the negative belief. In order to do this you must become aware of the negative emotion which then triggers the negative belief, while it is occurring and reprogram your belief system from negative to positive. This stops the ensuing bad habit in its tracks.

One of the keys to breaking bad habit is awareness of the triggers that set them off. Identifying the external triggers that set a habit in motion will empower you to break bad habits.

Some examples:

Bad Habit	Triggers
Eating too much fast food	McDonald's arches, watching TV, snacking habit
Smoking Cigarettes	Access to cigarettes, drinking alcohol, friends, time of day
Gambling	Advertisement, driving by convenience store, having a bookee, friends
Watching too much TV	Time of day

Understanding what triggers your habits requires that you become aware of the habits you have as well as the triggers that set those habits in motion. Awareness is the key. Without awareness, habit change is impossible.

HOW BELIEFS AND EMOTIONS AFFECT HABITS

Beliefs can either create wealth or create poverty. If you believe you are smart, you are right. If you believe you are dumb, you are right. If you believe life is an oyster, you are right. If you believe life is a struggle, you are right. What we believe determines who we become in life.

Our beliefs are stored deep in the subconscious mind. The subconscious part of the brain makes up 80% of brain mass. The other 20% is the conscious part of the brain. This 80% controls the autonomic system, directs behavior, stores habits and, finally, is where our emotions and our beliefs reside.

Most of the sensory information we take in every day is never picked by our pre-frontal cortex (conscious mind). Every day we are bombarded with an enormous amount of data taken in by our five senses. The hippocampus and Reticular Activating System (part of the subconscious) sees or captures all of this sensory information but intentionally does not share it with the conscious mind. This is so the conscious mind does not get overwhelmed, causing it to go into overload and shut down mode (meaning sleep). Instead, the subconscious filters what information the conscious mind sees, by way of the Reticular Activating System (RAS). The RAS allows in only certain, specific information. The information allowed into the conscious mind represents three types:

1. Information necessary for survival
2. Information related to dreams and goals and
3. Information related to our beliefs.

When it comes to survival, the conscious mind picks up a threat through one of its senses and instantaneously relays the potential threat to the hippocampus and amygdalae. If the threat is real, the conscious mind is taken offline during fight or flight and the limbic system and brain stem (part of the subconscious mind) instantly notify the cerebellum (controls motion) to get moving. You see the aftermath of this when victims of some life-threatening accident are said to be in a state of shock because they are unresponsive. What's really happening is their pre-frontal cortex is still in shut down mode and the subconscious is running things.

When we pursue dreams and goals, the RAS alerts the conscious mind about certain information it came into contact with, which it perceived as critical in helping us realize those dreams or achieving those goals. When it comes to dreams and goals, the subconscious mind communicates with the conscious mind through intuition and hunches. We call this the voice inside your head.

With regard to beliefs, the RAS shares information it has taken in which it perceives as consistent with our beliefs. Beliefs represent emotionalized thought programming the subconscious mind has accepted. Each belief represents a mini computer program that came about due to some emotional event. Our beliefs create the lives we live. If we are unhappy with our current financial circumstances, we need to change our beliefs. Our beliefs and our emotions play an important role in habit formation. A belief is formed two ways:

- Through internal and external programming – Self talk (internal) and statements made by others (external) that we have accepted as the truth.

- Through life events anchored in strong emotions.

The people closest to us, our parents, friends, teachers, coaches, etc., are the primary source of many of our beliefs. Some of these beliefs are formed by positive feedback and some are formed by negative feedback. This feedback sticks when it triggers strong positive or negative emotions. If the emotions we experience at the time of the feedback are strong enough, it gives birth to a belief which then alters our behavior: "Tom's a great tennis player". I heard that often and at an early age and it infused me with enormous emotion. As a result I practiced seven to eight hours every day during the summer and hit balls against my basement wall during the winter. Beliefs can also alter your behavior negatively. "You're an idiot. If your head wasn't attached to your neck you'd forget it somewhere".

That last line was spoken to me by my Dad, out of anger,

when I was just nine years old. I remember where it was said, when it was said and how it made me feel – stupid. It became a belief because of the powerful negative emotion I felt at the time it was said. Once I accepted that belief, it triggered all sorts of bad behavior that eventually became bad habits. I stopped doing homework, stopped paying attention in school and stopped participating in class. Why do homework, pay attention or participate in school? I'm too stupid to get an A. My new limiting belief eventually caused me to hate school. School only reminded me of my belief - that I was stupid. As a result of accepting this new limiting belief, I adopted habits that caused me to struggle academically for many years.

But the amazing thing about beliefs is that, no matter how ingrained they are, they can be changed. You don't have to be stuck with them forever, as I discovered in the 8th grade. This was when I met Ms. Summers. Ms. Summers was my eighth grade science teacher. She was so pretty and so nice. All the boys in the class had a crush on her, including myself. Early into the eighth grade, I was, surprise, surprise, failing science. After failing yet another test, Ms. Summers asked me to stay after class. She wanted to speak to me. I had gotten used to this routine: fail a test, stay after school and have to endure thirty minutes of teachers telling me Unfortunately, staying after class had become, for me, a regular occurrence. I just assumed I was going to get another lecture about not working hard, being an underachiever, etc. Instead, Ms. Summers told me that she believed I was actually very smart and that my problem was that I didn't believe in myself. She did, she said. She believed, if I wanted to, I could get the highest grade on the next test. In fact, Ms. Summers went one step further. She told me she believed I was going to get the best grade on the next test.

I remember going home on the bus that day and all I was thinking about was studying for my science test, which was three days away. I studied every night for three days for that damn test. I never studied so hard. I still remember those three days like it was yesterday because of what happened next. When Ms. Summers handed me my test results, in big black numbers was "99". I had received the second highest grade in the class, a 99. I couldn't ever remember getting a 99 on a test. Ms. Summers then called me to the front of the class and spent, what seemed like an hour, telling everybody in my class how smart I was. The emotion, the elation that I felt in not only getting the second highest score, but in how Ms. Summers made me feel, is still with me to this day. I felt smart. Ms. Summers was able to shatter my limiting belief because of the strong emotions I felt after doing so well on the test. Ms. Summers caused that emotion by making such a fuss with me in front of the entire class. One person's words changed my life forever because it created new emotional thought programming, also known as a belief. And it all happened in the course of just three days.

I went on to become a solid B+ student the rest of my eighth grade and into high school and college. I was even able to pass the CPA exam, get a Master's degree in taxation, and passed the Certified Financial Planning test, a ten hour exam, on the first try. The new belief, that I was smart, changed my study habits for the rest of my life.

Your daily habits are determined by your beliefs. If you believe you are smart, you will form good study habits and listening habits. If you believe you are stupid you will form bad study habits and poor listening habits. Once a belief is accepted, the brain creates habits around that belief in order to streamline activities and behaviors. If you have bad daily habits, the cause is your negative, limiting beliefs. If you have good daily habits it is because you have strong positive beliefs driving those good habits.

Parents, teachers, company managers and anyone in the position of authority has the capacity to eliminate the negative, limiting beliefs and bad habits of their children, students and employees. We all need to positively inspire everyone we are in a position to influence. One person can change the entire life of another person by simply altering their beliefs, which will, in turn, rid them of their bad daily habits forever.

Below is a list of some of the limiting beliefs that are creating bad habits and holding you back in life:

- Poor people can't become rich.

- Rich people have good luck and poor people have bad luck.

- I am not smart.

- I am ugly.

- I never have enough money.

- I can't do anything right – Everything I try I fail at.

- People don't like me.

- I'm disorganized and have no discipline.

- I'm not good at… fill in the blank. School, cooking, work, reading, relationships, math, science, reading, remembering things, etc.

- I'm fat because I can't lose weight.

Each one of these limiting beliefs is an individual mini computer program which alters your behavior in a negative way. These limiting beliefs are responsible for the life you have. If you are unhappy and want to change your circumstances in life you need to replace these limiting beliefs with positive, uplifting beliefs. It can be done. Here are some powerful strategies that will reprogram your subconscious and completely transform your life. If you follow these strategies for 30 days, the reprogramming will stick and you will shift your mindset from negative to positive.

The Future Letter

Writing the Future Letter is a lot of fun. It will really get your imagination going. When you're done, you will immediately feel better about yourself. Kids particularly enjoy this activity because it requires the use of imagination. Here's how it works:

Go into the future five, ten or twenty years. Let's use five years for purposes of this example. Imagine it is five years from now and you are writing a letter to yourself explaining what your life is like. In a perfect world, what would you like your life to look like five years from now? You want to paint a picture of your life, five years from now, that is the perfect, ideal life. It is the life you would want to have if you could snap your fingers today. Describe in your letter where you live, what kind of house you live in, what car you drive, what you do for a living, how much money you make, etc. Describe what you've done the past five years; the goals you've accomplished and the dreams that have come true. This Future Letter will become the blueprint for your future, perfect life.

Write Your Obituary

This exercise forces you to evaluate your current life and gives you an opportunity to re-write your script for the future. What would you like your perfect obituary to say? How would you like the world to remember you? Include all of the things you would like to accomplish in your life. Don't skimp. List all of the big dreams you realized in your life. Your obituary should make you feel in awe of your life. Really lay it on. Pour out your greatness. Paint a picture of the amazing person you were in life. Like the Future Letter, let this Obituary become the blueprint for your new, amazing life.

Make a List of Your Dreams and Wishes From Your Future Letter and Obituary

List every wish or dream that you find in your Future Letter and Obituary. Then reduce it to the top five wishes or dreams you would like to come true over the next five years. I'll cover this in more detail in Part IV.

Create Goals around Your Dreams and Wishes

Goals turn dreams into reality. Only after you've defined your dreams or wishes does the Goal-Setting process begin. 55% of the millionaires in my study set goals around their dreams and wishes. I'll cover this too in more detail soon.

PART II
TYPES OF
HABITS

KEYSTONE HABITS VS. ORDINARY HABITS

There are two types of habits:

1. Ordinary Habits and

2. Keystone Habits

Ordinary Habits are simple, basic, standalone habits; the time you wake up in the morning, the route you take to work, how you hold a fork, etc. Keystone Habits are more unique habits. They are unique because they affect other ordinary habits. Keystone Habits act like pac men; they move around searching for and overpowering other ordinary habits. Adopting Keystone Habits is the key to massive habit change. Let me give you an example:

It's New Year's Day and one of your resolutions is to lose weight. You're about 50 pounds overweight. A close friend, who is a runner, says the fastest way to lose weight is to run. So you decide to start running (Keystone Habit). You hate running, but after doing it a little while you're down fifteen pounds. One night you attend a social event and someone you know compliments you on your weight loss and tells you how amazing your look. You go home that night feeling happy, like you're floating on air. That compliment triggered an emotion inside of you and really got you pumped up. The next morning you decide to cut back on junk food (Ordinary Habit) and stop overeating (Ordinary Habit). You decide to run more in order to lose more weight, so you cut back on smoking (Ordinary Habit). Adopting just one Keystone Habit, running, had a domino effect, causing the elimination of three Ordinary Habits: junk food, overeating and smoking cigarettes. That's why Keystone Habits are unique and so powerful.

THE MANY SHADES
OF HABITS

Every habit results in an outcome. Some habits cause happiness, sadness, financial success, poverty, good health, bad health, short of long lifespans. There are also habits that alter our IQs, and which affect: relationships, job performance, motor skills, emotions or our overall circumstances in life. In this chapter we'll tackle some of the major habit categories.

Happiness Habits

You know happiness when you feel it. By definition, happiness is the sustained absence of negative emotions and an ongoing presence of positive emotions. Neurotransmitters are chemicals released when one or more neurons (brain cells) communicates with other neurons. Dopamine is the neurotransmitter for happiness. It is one of sixty neurotransmitters produced by the brain. When neurons release dopamine, it creates a sensation that we call happiness. When our dopamine level drop below a certain baseline, it creates a sensation we call sadness. If dopamine levels stay below that baseline for more than a few days, we call that depression. Depression is devastating to your health and causes a reduction in energy, which impairs productivity and creativity. When we are depressed, we pull back and retreat from life. We become listless and lose all interest in life. Almost all activities cease. We isolate ourselves from others. Depression affects one out of every eight individuals. It is a widespread, common affliction that affects hundreds of millions of people each year. It's critical, therefore, to engage in habitual physical or thinking activities that maintain or elevate our dopamine baseline in order to prevent sadness and depression from wreaking havoc with our lives.

What are these physical and thinking activities that increase our dopamine levels and vanquish sadness and depression?

- *Daily exercise* - Human beings are genetically hardwired for motion. Exercise sets in motion a domino effect of chemical reactions within the body. We'll get into the importance of exercise in more detail shortly.

- *Daily learning* - We are genetically hardwired to learn. The brain likes novelty. Our inborn natural curiosity is why we are explorers and inventors. Our brain likes it when it's put to use learning new things. When we learn something new, our brains release BDNF, a nerve growth factor that is like miracle grow for brain cells, along with the neurotransmitters dopamine and serotonin. These happiness chemicals are our brain's reward to us for helping it grow brain cells. Reading every day to learn is one of the most powerful happiness activities we can engage in.

- *Growing Constructive Relationships* - Human interaction is critical to happiness. More importantly, being in good company, surrounding ourselves with other upbeat, optimistic people, elevates our dopamine and oxytocin (another powerful happiness neurotransmitter) levels. Being alone or associating with negative types of people reduces the production of dopamine and oxytocin. Worse, these relationships create stress, which depresses our immune system. A depressed immune system reduces our resistance to colds and infections, causes plaque to build up in our arteries which leads to heart disease and turns on various genes that can lead to cancer. Making a habit out of associating with other happy people makes us happy and healthy.

- *Practiced Positivity* - Many studies have shown that making a habit of being upbeat, positive and optimistic makes people happier and more successful in school, sporting activities and in our business or careers. How do you make a habit of positivity? Start your day off with five minutes of meditation. Meditation reduces stress and repairs the physiological damage caused by stress. When we meditate, our brains release healthy neuro-chemicals such as serotonin, dopamine and endorphins. These chemicals trigger positive emotions and produce feelings of euphoria and happiness. Blood pressure drops during meditation and reboots the parasympathetic nervous system, which gets digestion back on track. Five to twenty minutes of meditation a day will do the trick. So how do you go about meditating? There are many variations, but simple is always better. Close your eyes and count to one hundred. See each number. Let all thoughts pass by like railroad cars along a track. After you finish your count, visualize your ideal, perfect life. See yourself living this perfect life, with your perfect family, perfect friends, perfect job and perfect house. See all of your financial worries disappear. See all of your goals and dreams being realized. If you can do this twice a day, once upon waking and once prior to sleep, that is best. All the negative physiological effects of stress will be offset by mediating. You will be better able to think and cope with your day to day responsibilities. Other positivity habits include: engaging in inspirational reading, reading positive affirmations, reviewing your "dream wish list" or reading a script of your ideal perfect future life. These daily activities prep your mind for positivity and lift your dopamine levels immediately.

Financial Success Habits

It takes time to become a self-made millionaire. Eighty percent of the self-made millionaires in my study became wealthy after age fifty. Somewhere along the line these self-made millionaires learned the secrets to saving and spending. In most cases either stumbled upon some mentor or read some book or watched some T.V. program or listened to some radio program that gave them the secret habits on saving and spending. Most, unfortunately, never learn about those habits. The vast majority of people never learn about these habits and spend their retirement years in abject poverty. But that's not you because you decided to invest your time and money in this book. And I intend on giving you your money's worth. In fact, if you learn nothing from this book but what follows, you will retire wealthier than 95% in the world. So let's get started and dive in. What are some of these savings and spending habits?

Category #1 Savings Habits:

Self-made millionaires make a habit of saving. The more you are able to save at an early age, the more wealth you'll accumulate. The self-made millionaires in my study all set the goal of saving 10-20% of their income during their pre-millionaire years. I uncovered a very unique Savings Habit strategy during my research that helped transform 175 ordinary individuals into self-made millionaires. I call it The Bucket System Savings Strategy. There are three steps to the Bucket System:

Step #1 – Allocate Savings by Category into four buckets:

- *Bucket #1* = Retirement Savings Bucket – This includes 401(k) plans, IRAs and other retirement plans or retirement-specific products (i.e. annuities).

- *Bucket #2* = Specific Expense Bucket – This includes a separate checking account, savings account, money market account or education savings account (i.e. 529 Plan) for major future expenses such as education costs for you or a child, wedding costs, costs associated with the birth of a child, home down payment, etc.

- *Bucket #3* = Unexpected Expense Bucket – This includes a separate checking account, savings account or money market account for expenses such as wedding gifts, medical costs, sudden loss of income (unemployment, medical issues or birth of a child), etc.

- *Bucket #4* = Cyclical Expense Bucket – This includes a separate checking account, savings account or money market account for birthday gifts, holiday expenses (Christmas, New Year's), vacation costs, back to school costs, etc.

You'll need to set up at least one retirement account and three different bank accounts (one for Buckets 2, 3 and 4). If you're saving for education costs for you or your child, you may want to set up one 529 plan for you or your child.

Step #2 – Establish Savings Goals

In order to make the Bucket System work, you need to establish the overall amount of savings you are able to set aside each pay period. For example, 10% of your net pay check. Then you need to allocate this 10% into each bucket as follows:

- 5% (50% of overall savings) into Bucket #1

- 2% (20% of overall savings) into Bucket #2

- 1.5% (15% of overall savings) into Bucket #3 and

- 1.5% (15% of overall savings) into Bucket #4

Step #3 – Automate the Savings Process

This is where the rubber meets the road – implementation. Automatically direct each of the above savings amounts into each bucket's separate account via automatic withdrawal from your net pay. You will need to instruct your payroll company to set up the automatic funding for each of the four bucket accounts. The payroll company will then automatically send each specific savings bucket amount to the custodial account or bank account that will be accumulating these amounts for you.

That's it. Pretty simple, right? "But I don't make enough to save," you say. Well, I'm here to help. In the next section, I'll show you how to cut your spending in order to be able to find the money you'll need to save.

Category #2 Spending Habits:

You'll never get rich if you spend more than you make. Here's a list of ten strategies that will help you manage your spending and increase your savings:

1. *Track Spending* – I like to call this spending awareness. Knowing where your money is going gives you control over your finances. You may find you are paying for things you are not using, such as club memberships or subscriptions.

2. *Periodically Audit Expenses* – Many expenses can change over time. Insurance costs often change. They can go up or down over time. Make sure you are paying the lowest insurance rates for homeowners, auto and life insurance. Cable and Internet costs can increase without you being aware of it. Calling your cable or Internet provider to secure the lowest fees available should be an annual process. Periodically shop cell phone plans. Increased competition in the cell phone industry is driving down monthly rates. Make sure you are not paying more than you have to.

3. *Purchase Good Quality Used Cars* – New cars lose value as soon as they come off the lot. Buying good quality used cars allows you to take advantage of this loss in value anomaly prevalent in the auto industry. 44% of the rich in my study purchased good quality used cars. Typically these are cars coming off a lease. They may be two or three years old. At 125,000 miles most cars will require some annual repairs. Expect to incur about $1,500 a year in repair costs when you hold on to cars beyond this 125,000 mileage mark. That is still significantly less than you would spend on a loan or lease for a new car.

4. ***Refinance Your Mortgage and Home Equity Loans*** – Are you paying the lowest rate possible on your mortgage? Do you have a home equity loan with a high rate of interest that you can roll into your new mortgage? Can you roll your student loans into your new mortgage?

5. ***Use Coupons*** – Even the wealthy in my study engaged in this money savings habit. 30% of the rich used coupons to buy food. Why pay more than you have to on groceries or other expenses?

6. ***Shop at Goodwill Stores*** – Many goodwill stores carry high quality clothing. You may have to spend a few extra bucks on tailoring, but it is well worth the additional cost. Don't let your ego get in the way. Thirty percent of the rich people in my study didn't.

7. ***Downsize Your Home or Apartment*** – For most, a home or apartment is the most expensive part of the spending budget. Downsizing into a less expensive home or apartment will save you thousands of dollars in interest, taxes and repairs every year. Keeping your housing costs to below 30% of your monthly net pay should be the goal.

8. ***Bargain Shop*** – Far too many make spontaneous purchases, paying much more than they otherwise would. That's a Poverty Habit. Shopping for bargains and taking advantage of sales events is a smart money habit.

9. ***Stick to BYOBs*** – There are many restaurants that do not sell alcohol, beer or wine and allow you to bring your own spirit of choice into their restaurant. Restaurants markup liquor sales by as much as 100%.

10. ***Vacation at Timeshares*** – Here's the deal – those who sell timeshares significantly discount the cost of a 3-5 day vacation in order to get you into their timeshare. Your only obligation is to sit through a 2-3 hour sales pitch. Sure, it's a nuisance but it can cut your vacation costs down by 50% or more. Is 2-3 hours of suffering through a sales pitch worth a $1,000?

Below are some specific guidelines on how much to spend on ordinary living expenses:

- Pay yourself first - Save 10-20% of your net income before you pay anyone else.

- Never charge ordinary living expenses on a credit card – If you can't meet your ordinary living expenses and must resort to the use of a credit card, you are by definition, living beyond your means. Accumulating credit card debt is the third leading cause of bankruptcy, behind a job loss and medical costs.

- Spending less than 30% of your net income on housing costs. Housing costs include rent, mortgage, real estate taxes, utilities, insurance, repairs and maintenance.

- Spending less than 15% of your net income on food. This includes groceries and

- does not include prepared food. Prepared food is part of your entertainment budget.

- Spending less than 10% of your net income on entertainment/gifts. This category includes bars, restaurants, movies, music, books, gifts, etc. Eating out and any prepared food you purchase is part of your entertainment budget.

- Spending less than 5% of your net income on car expenses. Car expenses include a lease, loan, insurance, gas, tolls, registration fees, repairs and maintenance.

- Spending less than 5% of your net pay on vacations.

- Avoid gambling. If you're going to gamble it should come out of your entertainment budget.

- Don't go over the top on gift giving. Gifts are part of your entertainment/gift budget. Sticking to your 10% entertainment budget will prevent you from going overboard on gift giving.

- Spending less than 5% on clothing. More than a few of the wealthy in my study had the Rich Habit of buying the bulk of their clothes at goodwill or consignment stores. Many Goodwill stores sell high quality clothing at a deep discount. It may require spending a few more dollars on a tailor, but it's well worth the additional cost.

- Spontaneous spending is never a good idea. You need to take the emotion out of your spending habits. There is always time to plan and shop before your spend your hard earned money.

Maintain a spending budget for all of the above spending categories and get into the habit of writing down everything you spend for thirty days. This will open your eyes to how much you actually spend. Real spending is always a very different dollar amount than imagined spending. You will be shocked to find out how much you spend on certain budget categories. And that's a good thing. Getting control of your spending is not an easy task. Once it becomes a daily habit, however, it gets much easier. You will fall into a pattern and a routine that will keep you out of the poor house, enable you to save and put you on the path to financial independence down the road.

Pretty amazing stuff isn't it? When you have knowledge, it empowers you and enables you to change your life. But I'm only warming up. There's a lot more I'm going to share with you that will rock your world and set you on the path to success and happiness.

Health Habits

Maintaining your health is critical to living a long, healthy, positive and energetic life. Here's a list of the healthy habits that will get you there:

- ***Daily Exercise*** - Exercise triggers the release of hormones known as endorphins and also the release of dopamine and serotonin, two powerful neurotransmitters. These chemicals all work in tandem in changing our mood and emotions from negative to positive. If we exercise daily, it is virtually impossible for depression to take root. Daily exercise also reduces stress. Running, jogging, walking, biking, lifting weights, etc. keep us healthy, happy and energetic. When we feel stress, there is a domino effect of physiology that takes place inside our bodies. When we feel stress, the hypothalamus increases the release of epinephrine and norepinephrine. These hormones make the heart beat faster and prepare the body for fight or flight. If the stress lingers, a gene on chromosome 10, called CYP17, is activated. This gene goes to work to convert cholesterol to cortisol. One of cortisol's side effects, unfortunately, is that it depresses the immune system by reducing the production of lymphocytes – white blood cells. The gene CYP17 also turns on another gene called TCF, which suppresses the creation of a protein called interleukin 2. Interleukin 2's purpose is to put white blood cells on high alert. White blood cells are our main defense against viruses, diseases, germs and any parasites that infect the body. Long-term stress, therefore, makes us more susceptible to disease. Daily exercise stops the this cortisol conversion process in its tracks, thus reducing stress.

- ***Healthy Eating*** - Making a daily habit of eating more nutritious food and consuming less junk food and alcohol, improves our well-being, provides adequate protein to the body, keeps our good and bad cholesterol in balance, reduces our blood-sugar levels and prevents obesity. Certain supplements such as Vitamin D3 improve our immune system. Turmeric has been shown in various studies to thwart cancer. Vitamins E and C are free radical sponges. They help rid cells of toxic free radicals. Free radicals, if left unchecked, can damage cell walls and create genetic mutations when they collide with the DNA that resides inside the nucleus of every cell in the body. Genetic mutations can lead to cancer. Eating right and reducing the number of calories we consume to less than 2,000 calories a day, helps maintain our health by reducing the accumulation of fat. Fat stores toxins in our bodies. Less fat means less toxins. If you are unsure if you are eating too much, one way to find out is to track what you eat each day, for thirty days. Thirty days of tracking the type of food and the number of calories you consume will open your eyes. How much you think you're eating will differ greatly from what you're actually eating. See the appendix for a copy of the Rich Habits Tracking Schedule to help you with your tracking. Tracking will help you understand how much junk food you are consuming each day. Ideally, you want to keep your junk food calories to under 300 per day. You want to make a habit of eating more fish, more vegetables, more salads, and healthy meats such as chicken and turkey. Avoid unhealthy meats such beef, ham, bacon, hot dogs and sausage. Unhealthy meats impair our cardiovascular system, elevate bad cholesterol, increase accumulation of fat and are high in calories. Also, while more expensive, organic food does not have any pesticides. Pesticides are carcinogens (cancer-causing chemicals).

Habits That Grow Your Brain and IQ

Neuroscience (the study of the brain), over the past ten years, has completely changed our understanding of how the brain works. We now know that the brain changes every day. We can rewire our brains (called neuroplasticity) throughout our entire lives and even well into our eighties. We also now know that the hippocampus gives birth to thousands of new neurons every day (called neurogenesis). Thanks to the study of, and mapping of the genome, we've discovered that turning on certain genes can help increase our IQs during our lifetime. We know that IQ can change over time. IQs are not fixed. Just because you were a "C" student at age seventeen with an IQ of 100 doesn't necessarily mean you will stay that way. You can increase your IQ all during your life.

Self-made millionaires do certain things every day that continuously improve their brains and increase their intelligence during their lifetimes. These activities increase brain mass by increasing and strengthening old neural connections and by creating entirely new neural connections. Let's touch on some of the brain-building activities of self-made millionaires:

- *Daily Learning* - Every time you learn something new, you re-wire your brain. New neurons are recruited and begin firing with one another (known as synapses). As new neural pathways are created by learning, your brain actually increases in size; your intelligence grows. Eighty eight percent of the wealthy in my study, long before they struck it rich, formed the daily habit of engaging in thirty minutes or more of self-education reading. This single, simple daily habit alone, helped them to increase their cognitive abilities, which contributed to their success much later in life.

- *Daily Aerobic Exercise* - Aerobic exercise floods the bloodstream with oxygen. This oxygen eventually makes its way to the brain. Oxygen acts like a sponge inside the brain. It soaks up free radicals (cancer causing elements) and converts these free radicals to carbon dioxide. The blood carries this carbon dioxide to the lungs, which then removes the carbon dioxide from our bodies by exhaling it into the environment. The more we exercise, the more oxygen we take in and the more free radicals are soaked up by this oxygen sponge process. Aerobic exercise also reduces the incidence of obesity, heart disease, high blood pressure, type 2 diabetes, stroke and certain types of cancer. Twenty to thirty minutes of aerobic exercise every day has been proven to stimulate the growth of axons and axon branches on each neuron. Recent neurological studies have found a correlation between the number of axons and axon branches inside your brain and intelligence. More axons and axon branches translates into higher intelligence. Aerobic exercise also increases the release of neurotrophins, or Nerve Growth Factor (NFG). NFG stimulates the growth of neurons, helps maintain a healthy coating around every neuron (called the myelin sheath) and improves communication (synaptic communication) between neurons. Increased synaptic communication translates into better memory and faster recall. So, daily aerobic exercise feeds the brain, cleans the brain and increases your intelligence, each and every time you engage in it. Aerobic exercise also boosts your high-density cholesterol lipoprotein (HDL or "good cholesterol") and lowers your low-density lipoprotein cholesterol (LDL or "bad cholesterol"). The result? Less buildup of plaque in your arteries. Studies show that people who participate in regular aerobic exercise live longer than those who don't exercise regularly. Healthier people have fewer sick days, more energy and this translates into more productivity at work. More productivity makes you more valuable to your organization, customers or clients, which translates into more money. Long-term stress impairs our immune system's ability to fight off viruses, diseases, germs and parasites. Because aerobic exercise floods the body with oxygen, this increased oxygen reduces the effects of stress on the body. Aerobic exercise is like a double in baseball; it reduces the effects of stress while at the same time reducing stress itself.

- **_Drink Alcohol in Moderation_** - Our livers are able to process about two ounces of alcohol an hour (about two tweltve ounce glasses of beer an hour). Anything in excess of that, allows alcohol to enter your bloodstream which is then carried to your brain. Once alcohol reaches the brain, it infiltrates the glutamate receptors in your synapses, damaging the neurons' ability to fire off signals. If you regularly drink in excess, you are causing long-term damage to these receptors and this can cause permanent damage to your memory and your motor skills. Is it a coincidence that 84% of the wealthy in my study drank less than two ounces of alcohol a day? I don't think so. Their moderation in the consumption of alcohol helped them keep their brains healthy, growing and improving.

- **_Get a Good Night's Sleep_** – Eighty nine percent of the wealthy in my study slept an average of seven hours or more each night. Why is sleep so important to brain function? Everyone who sleeps goes through four to six sleep cycles a night. Each cycle lasts about ninety minutes. Each of these sleep cycles is composed of five separate levels of sleep: Alpha, theta, delta, rapid eye movement (REM) and then back to theta. For each individual sleep cycle, the first three sleep levels (alpha, theta and delta) last sixty-five minutes. REM lasts twenty minutes and the final level of sleep, theta, lasts five minutes. The number of hours you sleep is less important than the number of complete sleep cycles you have each night. Five complete sleep cycles a night is considered optimal. Completing less than four sleep cycles a night, however, negatively affects our health. REM sleep is particularly important, as its primary function appears to be long-term memory storage. During REM sleep, what we've learned the day before is transported to the hippocampus. If we do not complete at least four ninety minute sleep cycles a night, long-term memory storage becomes impaired. Completing at least four sleep cycles, the night after learning new information or a new skill, locks in the new information or new skill. If we get less than four complete nienty minute sleep cycles the night after learning anything, it's as if the learning never occurred. Sleep helps you remember what you learned yesterday.

- *Make a Habit of Engaging in New Activities* - Every time you engage in a new activity and then practice it, you grow your brain. When we regularly repeat new activities, the neurons communicating with each other begin to form a permanent neural pathway, thus growing the size of our brains. It is critical for older people to engage in new activities in order to keep their brains active and prevent shrinkage. Those who want to grow their brains should engage in a new activity and repeat it until it becomes a new skill. This can take anywhere from 18 days to 254 days. Each new activity that becomes a skill creates brain mass and keeps our minds active and our brains healthy.

- ***Weight Training 3 or More Days a Week*** - Neural stem cells (new brain cells) are born in the hippocampus and either divide into neural cells or glial cells (support cells for neurons). Neural cells are sent from the hippocampus to the dendrite gyrus, which acts like a traffic cop, ordering them to go to specific regions of the brain. Voluntary exercise increases the number of neural stem cells created by the hippocampus. Here's how it works: weight training delivers blood-soaked oxygen to the brain. The more you lift weights, the higher the blood flow. This increased blood flow then feeds the brain with more glucose (brain fuel) and oxygen (which removes free radicals from the brain like a sponge, in effect cleaning the brain). Weight training also increases the production of BDNF (Brain Derived Neurotrophic Factor) inside the hippocampus. BDNF is like miracle grow for the brain, helping it give birth to more neural cells. BDNF also helps increase the health and size of old neurons. In effect, weight training grows your brain by creating new brain cells and also by maintaining old brain cells. Every brain cell has one axon and multiple dendrites. The axon of each brain cell connects with the dendrites of other brain cells. This is called a synapse. There is a direct correlation between the number of axons and synapses an individual has and their intelligence. Lifting weights increases the growth of axons, which helps contribute to increased synaptic activity. Anything that increases the number of axons and synapses, therefore, increases intelligence.

Powerful Relationship-Building Habits

Self-made millionaires are very particular about who they associate with. Their goal is to develop relationships with other success-minded individuals. Eighty six percent of the self-made millionaires in my Rich Habits Study made a habit out of associating with other success-minded people. Some of the individual characteristics self-made millionaires seek include:

- Individuals who are financially successful.

- Individuals with good habits.

- Individuals who are positive, upbeat and optimistic.

- Individuals who are calm and happy.

- Individuals who are able to get along with others.

- Individuals who do not gossip about others.

- Individuals who inspire and motivate.

- Individuals who are enthusiastic.

- Individuals who take personal responsibility for their lives.

At the same time, self-made millionaires also make an effort to eliminate toxic relationships. Toxic relationships have some of the following individual characteristics:

- Individuals who are always experiencing some type of turmoil.

- Individuals with bad habits.

- Individuals who are negative, perpetually depressed, unhappy or pessimistic.

- Individuals who are constantly putting out fires.

- Individuals who are perpetually fighting with someone.

- Individuals who gossip.

- Individuals who are dream killers.

- Individuals who lack enthusiasm.

- Individuals with a victim mindset.

- Individuals who blame others for their problems.

Eighty percent of the self-made millionaires in my Rich Habits Study used four relationship building strategies to grow and strengthen their relationships:

1. *Hello Call* - The Hello Call is used primarily to gather information on each contact.

2. *Happy Birthday Call* - The Happy Birthday Call keeps your relationships on life support. At least once a year you are forced to reach out to your contacts to wish them a happy birthday. About 5-10% of these contacts will reciprocate and call you on your birthday, taking your relationship off life support.

3. *Life Event Call* - The Life Event Call is the most powerful strategy because it puts your relationships on steroids. This is a call you make to acknowledge some life event: birth, death,

engagement, marriage, health issue, etc. Life Event Calls put your relationships on steroids. They grow the roots to the relationship tree deeper and faster than any other relationship-building strategy.

4. ***Networking/Volunteering*** - Networking & Volunteering allows you to meet new people and offers the opportunity to showcase your skills in a safe, friendly and stress-free environment. Developing a networking process is critical to success. When you network the right way, you gain customers, clients, strategic business partners, followers and networking partners and this translates into more money. Self-made millionaires are master networkers. Their networking efforts are intended to grow their association with other successful individuals.

There are a number of ways these millionaires go about networking:

- They join networking groups/clubs. BNI International is the most popular, but many self-made millionaires often organized their own unique networking groups.

- They joined advisory boards of community businesses.

- They joined local civic groups such as the Lions Club, Rotary Club, Chambers of Commerce, Knights of Columbus, Optimist Club or local business groups.

- They did speaking engagements. Speaking engagements are probably the most efficient networking tool available. One speaking engagement can mean thirty or more potential clients/customers or new relationships. Many individuals fear public speaking. One of the common traits among these millionaires is their ability to overcome their fears. Public speaking sets you apart from the masses. It is a competitive advantage.

- They join non-profit groups and eventually get on the board or run one or more committees. Non-profit groups are a very valuable resource for referrals. It allows you an opportunity to showcase your skills and develop long-lasting relationships. Referrals come from every direction; fellow members, vendors, donors and beneficiaries of the organization. Most board members on non-profits are very successful, wealthy individuals who have strong, powerful relationships. Joining a non-profit grants you access to this treasure trove of valuable relationships of the other volunteers.

When self-made millionaires find someone special, they devote an enormous amount of their time and energy into building a strong relationship with them. Their goal is to grow each new relationship from a sapling into a redwood. They used the Law of Reciprocity to very rapidly turn their new relationships into redwoods. Here's how this law works: each day you dedicate a portion of your day to improving the life of just one of your valued relationships.

Spend time each day helping your relationship achieve their goals, improve their careers or grow their business. Thirty minutes a day is all it takes. Eventually your relationships will become your biggest cheerleaders, best salespeople and best referral source. This strategy also opens doors to new contacts. Successful people use the Law of Reciprocity every day.

RICH HABITS VS. POOR HABITS

Forty percent of all of our daily actions, thinking and choices are habits. Because habits represent unconscious behavior, most of us are unaware that our current life circumstances are the direct result of our habits. Many individuals live paycheck to paycheck, barely getting by. They either scratch their heads, wondering what they're doing wrong, or they play the victim, blaming others for their circumstances in life. The fact is, habits are behind all success and all failure. Habits create outcomes. The habits we pick up in life can be either good or bad habits. Good habits automatically put us on a path of success in life. Individuals with good habits do better in school, better at work, make more money, are happier, are healthier and have a longer life-span. Conversely, bad habits automatically put us on a path of failure in life. Individuals with bad habits do poorly in school, at work, make less money, are unhappy, unhealthy and have a shorter life-span.

Habits represent unconscious behaviors or thinking we engage in regularly. This is a good thing if those habits are good habits. Unconsciously, through our good habits, we are creating a good life: good financial health, good physical health, good mental health and an overall feeling of happiness. But if we have bad habits, we are creating a life with financial problems, health issues, depression and unhappiness.

From my research, I discovered that daily habits dictate how successful or unsuccessful you will be in life. By focusing my research on rich people ($160,000 income per year plus $3.2 million or more in net liquid assets) and poor people ($35,000 income or less per year plus less than $5,000 in net liquid assets) I was able to identify common habits possessed by the rich and the poor. This research is important because it gets to the heart of the cause of wealth and poverty. I learned eight key things from my study:

1. Daily habits represent 40% or more of all of our daily activities, our daily thinking and the daily choices or decisions that we make.

2. Certain habits are Keystone Habits. As I mentioned earlier, Keystone Habits are unique habits because they affect other ordinary habits. Keystone Habits have a domino effect on ordinary habits. They are the most powerful type of habit. They are also harder to adopt and harder to eliminate.

3. Certain habits are Ordinary Habits. They stand on their own and do not affect other habits. They are easier to adopt and easier to change.

4. There is a cause and effect associated with habits. Habits are the cause of wealth, poverty, happiness, sadness, stress, good relationships, bad relationships, good health or bad health. Habits impact our lives without our being aware of it.

5. Most of our habits come from our parents. They're generational, meaning they are passed along from one generation to the next.

6. Rich people have significantly more Rich Habits than they have Poor Habits.

7. Poor people have significantly more Poor Habits than they have Rich Habits.

8. All habits can be changed.

What are some of the Rich Habits and Poor Habits that are creating a good life or a bad life? In my bestselling book Rich Habits, I identified ten Keystone Habits that separate the rich from the poor. Here they are:

The Ten Rich Habits

1. I will create my own personal daily Rich Habits and follow them each day.

2. I will create goals and form habits around my goals.

3. I will read thirty minutes or more each day for self-education.

4. I will exercise thirty minutes or more aerobically each day.

5. I will devote part of my day strengthening relationships with other success-minded individuals.

6. I will live each day in a state of moderation.

7. I will accomplish 70% or more of my daily "to-do" list.

8. I will make an effort each day to be positive, enthusiastic and optimistic.

9. I will save 10% or more of everything I earn.

10. I will control my thoughts and emotions each day.

While these represent the ten core Keystone Rich Habits, in my five-year Rich Habits study, I identified over 300 behavior habits, thinking habits and decision-making habits that actually separate self-made millionaires from everybody else. I'd like to share with you some of that data. It will help shine a light on just how important habits are in shaping the life we currently have. I'd like to take you on a journey. We are going to take a walk in the footsteps of the wealthy. Together, we will peer into the minutia of their daily lives, in order to really see and understand the habits which helped transform their lives from ordinary to extraordinary. We will also take a walk in the footsteps of the poor, looking at their habits, because it's equally important to know which habits hold you back in life. You have to see both sides of the coin. I'm going to list each of the Rich Habits and Poor Habits by level of importance in shaping the lives of the rich and poor. Because no one has ever done a study like this, it's going to open up your eyes. Let's pull back the curtain on the habits of rich and poor. Let's be that fly on the wall to their lives. Remember, these habits are listed by the level of impact they have on the lives of the rich and poor.

Rich Habits - The Habits of Self-Made Millionaires

1. *Daily Self-Education Reading:* Eighty eight percent of the rich devote thirty minutes or more each day in self-education or self-improvement reading. Also, 63% listened to educational audiobooks or podcasts while commuting back and forth to work. Most did not read for entertainment. In fact, only 11% engage in any entertainment reading at all. The rich read to acquire or maintain knowledge. When they read, 58% read biographies of other successful people. There are important life lessons to be learned in biographies of people with rags to riches stories. Biographies expose the thinking habits, challenges, and ups and downs of its subjects. Biographies educate. Fifty five percent also read self-help or personal development books. These books share basic and novel ideas on improving your life in some way. They force you to evaluate what you're doing right and what you're doing wrong. Self-help books provide a sort of best practices for better living. Lastly, 51% of the rich read history books. By studying history, we are able to better understand life. History paints a picture of human triumphs and human failings. It's

like a compass, pointing us in the right direction, while also showing us the wrong direction.

2. Thirty Minutes or More of Daily Aerobic Exercise: Seventy six percent of the rich exercised thirty minutes or more every day aerobically. Aerobic exercise involves anything that's cardio. Running, jogging, walking, Stair Masters, elliptical, treadmill, biking, etc. Any exercise that gets the heart rate up above 120 beats per minute for a sustained period of time is cardio. Cardio not only is good for the body, but it's good for the brain. Cardio improves brain function. It grows the neurons (brain cells) in the brain. It feeds the brain with certain hormones, like Brain Derived Neurotrophic Factor (BDNF). BDNF is like Miracle Grow for brain cells. It helps them grow more dendrites and increases the size of axons, two critical components of brain cells. The more dendrites you have and the bigger your axons, the smarter you become. Cardio delivers more oxygen-soaked blood to the brain. Oxygen helps improve the functioning of brain cells. The more oxygen we take in through cardio exercise, the healthier our brains become. Exercise also increases the production of glucose. Glucose is brain fuel. The more fuel you feed your brain, the more it grows and the smarter you become.

3. *Build Relationships With Other Success-Minded People*: You are only as successful as those you frequently associate with. If you want to be more successful in life you need to surround yourself with other success-minded people. You also need

to minimize contact with toxic people. Successful people can open the door of opportunity to you with one phone call, email or meeting. You can find these success-minded people on boards and committees of nonprofit organizations. This is why so many wealthy people volunteer for charitable organizations, civic groups or trade groups. It helps them expand their network of other success-minded people. If you are not rich, volunteer. If you are unemployed, volunteer. If you hate your job, volunteer. The new relationships you will create will open the door to unexpected opportunities. Seventy two percent of the wealthy volunteered five hours or more each month. 86% of these self-made millionaires devoted time to building strong, long-term relationships with individuals who had a positive, upbeat mindset. The rich are always on the lookout for individuals who are goal-oriented, optimistic, enthusiastic and who have an overall positive mental outlook. They also make a point to limiting their exposure to toxic, negative people, which we've already touched on. One of the strategies I uncovered in my research, involved the rich spending more than one hour a week with their positive relationships and spending less than an hour a week with their toxic relationships. You want to maximize the time you spend with your success relationships and minimize the time you spend with your toxic relationships. To build these relationships, the rich do six things: #1 they make happy birthday calls, #2 they make hello calls, #3 they make life event calls, #4 they network #5 they volunteer and #6 they participate in formal or informal mastermind groups. Formal mastermind groups include trade groups, business groups and common interest groups. Informal groups include weekly or monthly meetings or phone calls with a select number of individuals who are all pursuing something in common, whether a similar goal, similar business or similar activity. The informal mastermind groups typically have no more than five or six participants. A real life example of this is found in the new car dealer industry. Many individual new car dealers, within the same franchise, make a habit of meeting quarterly to compare notes and share best practices.

4. *Pursue Your Own Goals:* Eighty percent of the wealthy in my study were obsessed with pursuing goals. Fifty five percent spent a year or more in pursuit of a single goal. Pursuing your own goals is the key. Too many make the mistake of pursuing someone else's goal. Parents, who want the best for us, may push us to become doctors, CPAs, attorneys or engineers. Many follow their parents' advice only to find out, years later, that they are unhappy and not making the money they thought they would make. I'm here to tell you to avoid putting your ladder on someone else's wall and then spending the best years of your life climbing it. Find your own wall, your own dreams, and your own goals and pursue them. They need to be yours and not someone else's. Only then will you find your true calling and some meaning in life. When

you pursue someone else's dreams or goals you may eventually become unhappy with your chosen profession. Your performance and compensation will reflect it. You will eke out a living, struggling financially. You simply won't have the passion that is necessary for success to happen. Passion makes work fun. Passion gives you the energy, persistence and focus needed to overcome failures, mistakes and rejection. It infuses you with a fanatical tenacity that makes it possible to overcome obstacles and pitfalls that block your path. According to my data, pursuing your own dreams and goals creates the greatest long-term happiness and results in the greatest accumulation of wealth. Those who pursue their own goals or life dreams, love what they do for a living and are the happiest people.

5. *Dream-Set Then Goal-Set:* There's actually a process to realizing your dreams. Unfortunately, many well-meaning personal development experts don't fully understand the process and, as a result, those who embrace their teachings soon find themselves discouraged and disillusioned when they fail to realize their dreams. The confusion is in misinterpreting Goal-Setting as the process to realizing your dreams. While Goal-Setting is part of the process, the actual foundation for realizing your dreams begins first with Dream-Setting. I'll explain this Dream-Setting – Goal-Setting Process in more detail in Part IV.

6. *Avoid Time Wasters:* When most people think of risk, they think of it in terms of some financial

investment they make: investing money in a new business, investing in stocks, gambling, playing the lottery, or lending someone money in exchange for some future financial gain. But financial risk is not the greatest risk you take. You can always earn more money. There is a risk that, when made, never returns. It's gone forever. The greatest risk we take is time. When we invest our time in anything, it's lost forever. It never gets renewed or returned to us. Yet, because we are all given, what seems to be an abundance of time, it has very little value. So we spend an enormous amount of our time engaged in wasteful activities, such as sitting in front of a T.V. for hours, commenting on Facebook, watching YouTube videos, sitting at a bar, lying in bed or engaged in some other non-productive activity. When we waste time, it's gone forever. We don't consider how precious time is until we are older and realize our time is running out. Time needs to be invested wisely, pursuing goals, dreams, or some major purpose in life. Any investment we make of our time should pay dividends down the road in the form of creating happiness events, financially security, creating a legacy or in helping improve the lives of others. When you see time as the greatest risk of all, it will force you to become more aware of exactly how you invest your time. Invest it wisely, because you will never get it back. Sixty seven percent of the self-made millionaires in my study watched less than one hour of T.V. each day. Sixty three percent spent less than one hour a day on the Internet (recreationally). This freed up time for them to pursue their goals, read, learn, exercise, volunteer and network.

7. **Sleep 7 - 8 Hours Each Day**: Eighty nine percent of the self-made millionaires in my study slept seven hours or more each day. Sleep is critical to success. Neuroscientists have made some incredible breakthroughs in the past ten years. One thing they continue to study is why we need to sleep. What they are discovering is fascinating. Sleep accomplishes so many things behind the scenes. One purpose of sleep is memory formation. During REM sleep, the hippocampus and neocortex send signals back and forth to each other thousands of times. This process creates memories. Another discovery is that sleep enables offline communication between the conscious mind (aka neocortex), which shuts down during sleep, and the subconscious mind (limbic system and brain stem). This is important because the subconscious mind is regularly taking in sensory data that is invisible to the conscious mind. When we experience intuition, this is actually the subconscious mind communicating something to the conscious during sleep. When you wake, the conscious mind, that voice inside your head, talks to you about what it learned from the subconscious mind while you slept. The average adult requires 7 1/2 hours of sleep each day, in five, ninety minute sleep cycles. Each of these five sleep cycles is composed of five separate levels of sleep: alpha, theta, delta, rapid eye movement (REM) and then back to theta. The first three sleep levels

last sixty five minutes. REM lasts twenty minutes and the final level of sleep lasts five minutes. The number of hours you sleep is less important than the number of complete sleep cycles you have when you sleep. Four sleep cycles is the minimum, while five sleep cycles is optimal.

8. *Get Up Early:* Forty four percent, or roughly half of the self-made millionaires in my study, woke at least three hours before their work day actually began. Why is getting up early so important to success? Life has a way of throwing wrenches into our day. How many of us raise our hands in frustration at the end of a work day because the three or four things we wanted to get done were somehow replaced by unanticipated disruptions. Unanticipated disruptions happen. Sometimes they happen too often. These disruptions have a psychological effect on us. They can drip into our subconscious and eventually form the belief that we have no control over our life. Once formed, this belief puts on its work hat, telling us, subconsciously, that we are not in control of our day. This belief causes us to feel helpless. Feeling helpless is the number one common cause of depression. But there's a solution. There's a way to take back control of your life and kill the roots to that negative belief. It's called the "Five AM Club". Getting up at five am to tackle the top three things you want to accomplish in your day allows you to regain control of your life. It gives you a sense of confidence that you direct your life. It gives you a

feeling of power over your life. It puts the reigns of "your'" life back into "your" hands. Getting up at 5am is a daily habit. It will take time to form this daily habit. This is one of those Keystone Habits I like to talk about. Keystone Habits are the most powerful type of habits because of the domino effect they have on other habits. One strategy to help you develop this Five AM Club habit, is to find someone to join your Five AM Club to hold you accountable. Someone who will be there, waiting and looking for you at five am. This will force you to overcome the urge to sleep in. Start your 5 am Club tomorrow. Find an accountability partner, someone who will join your Five AM Club. You'll regain control of your life and it will make you feel better about yourself. You'll gain confidence that life is within your control and it will end your feeling of helplessness.

9. ***Develop Multiple Streams of Income*** - Self-made millionaires do not rely on one singular source of income. They develop multiple streams. Three seemed to be the magic number in my study. Sixty five percent had three or more streams of income that they created prior to making their first million dollars. Diversifying sources of income allows you to weather the economic downturns that inevitably occur. These downturns are not as severe when you have multiple streams of income. Most people have "one pole in one pond" and when that single income stream is impacted by an economic downturn, they suffer financially.

Conversely, the rich have "several poles in different ponds" and are able to draw income from other sources when one source is temporarily impaired. Some of the additional streams include: real estate rentals, REITs, Tenants-in-common real estate investments, triple net leases, stock market investments, annuities, seasonal real estate rentals (beach rentals, ski rentals, lakefront rentals), private equity investments, part ownership in side businesses, financing investments, ancillary product or services and royalties (patents, books, oil, timber).

10. *Avoid Procrastination* - Procrastination is a Poor Habit. It prevents even the most talented individuals from realizing success in life. Most people have this Poor Habit, and it is not an accident that most people struggle financially in life. Success has many moving parts and procrastination is a big moving part. One of the main contributors to procrastination is not being passionate about what you do for a living. That's 87% of the working population in the world. According to Gallup, only 13 percent of employees are "engaged" in their jobs, or emotionally invested in their work and focused on helping their organizations improve. The data, which is based on nationally representative polling samples in 2011 and 2012 from more than 140 countries, showed that 63 percent are "not engaged"—or simply unmotivated and unlikely to exert extra effort—while the remaining 24 percent are "actively disengaged," or truly unhappy

and unproductive. Why? The reason is that we simply like to do the things we like to do and we put off the things we do not like to do. Whether you realize it or not, procrastination is a big reason why you are struggling financially in life. It damages your credibility with employers and fellow colleagues at work. It also affects the quality of your work and this affects the business you or your employer receive from customers, clients and business relationships. Procrastination brands you as someone who cannot be trusted or whose work product is poor. Worse, procrastination can lead to litigation, which causes stress and financial costs that can run into the thousands of dollars. Believe it or not, the voice of procrastination screams just as loud and clear in the minds of those who excel in life, as it does in the minds of those who do not. The difference is how successful people stop that voice of procrastination in its tracks. In my five-year study on the daily habits of the rich and poor, I uncovered five tools that can help anyone silence the voice of procrastination forever:

- *Tool #1 – To-do Lists* - Successful people rely on "to-do" lists to help them get things done. There are two types of daily to-dos:

  i. *Goal To-Dos* – These are daily tasks tied to monthly, yearly and long-term goals. These are almost always fixed in nature, meaning the same to-dos show up every day on the to-do list. For example: "Make Ten Telemarketing Phone Calls".

ii. ***Non-Goal To-Dos*** – These are to dos that are unrelated to any goals. They may be administrative tasks (i.e. Respond to Emails), client tasks (i.e. Meeting with Client) or daily obligations (i.e. Go to Bank). They may be fixed, daily tasks or they may vary daily.

- Tool #2 – The Daily Five - Every day, successful people incorporate into their daily "to-do" list five things to accomplish before the day ends. This is a particularly important tool for that 87% who are not passionate about their job. The Daily Five can represent five things that are unrelated to your 9-5 job. They can be five minor things that you do every day that move you forward toward accomplishing some goal or realizing some dream or purpose in life.

- ***Tool #3 – Setting and Communicating Artificial Deadlines*** - When you set deadlines and communicate those deadlines to third parties who are directly affected by your completion of a task, you increase the urgency for completing the task. It elevates it from a mere "to-do" to a personal promise you make to another individual. It puts pressure on you to fulfill your promise and meet the deadline.

- ***Tool #4 – Accountability Partners*** - An Accountability Partner is someone you meet with regularly (weekly, for example) who holds your feet to the fire in accomplishing your tasks. This can be one or more individuals. Knowing that there are others who will hold you accountable to perform certain tasks, elevates those tasks from mere "to-dos". We all perform better when we know others are watching.

- ***Tool #5 – "Do It Now" Affirmations*** - No one likes to be nagged. Nagging, whether we realize it or not, alters our behavior. We tend to get something done that we don't want to do when we are repeatedly nagged about it. The "Do It Now" affirmation is a self-nagging technique that works. By repeating the words "Do It Now" over and over again, we are effectively nagging ourselves. When I uncovered this tool during my research, I began using it to nag myself into doing things I regularly procrastinated on, like time and billing. Now all I have to do is think about the affirmation in order for the nagging to alter my behavior and force me to get that task done.

11. Find a Success Mentor – Ninety three percent of the self-made millionaires in my study, who had a mentor in life, attributed their enormous wealth to their mentors. Sixty eight percent said that the mentoring they received from others was a critical factor in their success. Success Mentors do more than simply influence your life in some positive way. They regularly and actively participate in your success by teaching you what to do and what not to do. They share with you valuable life lessons they learned either from their own mentors or from the school of hard knocks. Finding a mentor puts you on the fast track to wealth accumulation.

In my research I discovered five types of Success Mentors:

- *Parents* – Parents are often the only opportunity any of us have at having a mentor in life. Parents who are success mentors to their children help distance their kids from the competition. They set their children up for success as adults. This is why parenting is so critical to success in life. Teach your children good daily success habits. Doing so makes it highly unlikely that they will struggle in life financially.

- *Teachers* – Good teachers are good mentors. Teachers can reinforce the mentoring children receive at home from their parents, or step in to provide the much needed success mentoring, absent at home.

- *Career Mentors* – For those not fortunate enough to have had parents or teachers who provided success mentoring, finding someone at work who can act as a mentor is the fast track to wealth accumulation. They help you avoid making mistakes and will point you in the right direction. Find someone at work who you admire, trust and respect and ask them to be your mentor. They should be at least two levels above you at work.

- Book Mentors – Books can take the place of actual mentors. The best source for book mentors are biographies of self-made millionaires. 58% of the self-made millionaires in my study read biographies of other successful people.

- *Mentored by the School of Hard Knocks* – When you learn good daily success habits through the school of hard knocks you are essentially your own mentor. You teach yourself what works and what does not work. You learn from your mistakes and failures. This is the hard way because those mistakes and failures carry significant costs in both time and money. But this is also the most effective type of mentorship, because the lessons you learn are infused with emotion and never forgotten.

12. *Positive Mental Outlook* - Long-term success is only possible when you have a positive mental outlook. In my research, positivity was a hallmark of all of the self-made millionaires. Fifty four percent of the millionaires believed their optimism was a driving force in their success. Forty three percent believed they would one day be rich. Seventy nine percent believed they were the cause of their circumstances in life. Most of us are completely unaware of our thoughts. If you stop to listen to your thoughts, to be aware of them, you'd find most of them are negative. But you only realize you are having these negative thoughts when you force yourself to be aware of them. Awareness is the key. The new age term for this is mindfulness. Physiologically, these voices inside your head, emanates from an area of the brain called the amygdala. The amygdala resides in the limbic system portion of

the brain. It never stops talking to us. It's there for a purpose. Think of it as a radar system, warning us of danger. It broadcasts worry, fear and doubts as a means of protection, to keep us alert and on guard for danger, predators, unsavory people, etc. This voice whispers to us all sorts of things when we embark on some new, unchartered territory or anything that involves risk. The real-life triggers for this voice are setting goals, pursuing a dream, investing your money in a business or a project, a new job opportunity, a possible promotion with challenging responsibilities, getting married, getting divorced, buying a house, selling a house, moving to a new location, having a baby, going to college, taking up a new sport, etc. Sometimes this voice says things to us like:

- You could fail, lose money, get fired or go bankrupt.

- You could get hurt or injured.

- You'll embarrass yourself.

- It might not work out, it'll end in divorce, it could be a disaster.

- I'm not up to it, it's too much responsibility for me, what if I do a terrible job.

These negative voices are warnings to stop what we are doing and reverse course, back to our comfort zone. Most individuals give in to the voices. But I found a few who don't. These courageous individuals ignored those voices; pursuing goals, dreams, new business opportunities and new challenges in life. How? How come they didn't obey the voices inside their head? What do they do to overcome these voices and persist, while most everyone else stops in their tracks? The self-made millionaires in my study played the What If Game. The What If Game silences those negative voices inside your head. The What If Game diffuses the negative self-talk. It's like battery acid, melting away doubt, fear, anxiety and worry. In his book Think Like a Champion, Donald Trump explains how he shuts down his demon voices by playing the What If Game. When Trump is considering a new project, he confessed in his book that those demon voices came charging in like an army. Many of the demon voices come from inside his head, but many of them also come from individuals who work with Trump. In the early phases of pursuing a new project these voices warn him of all sorts of dangers. When he was in the evaluation phase of what became his award winning T.V. show, The Apprentice, Trump was confronted with an overwhelming number of demon voices advising him to stop:

- The show might fail. If the show is a flop, it will damage the Trump brand.

- It will distract me from my current business. My core businesses would suffer financially.

- What if the show turns people against me?

- What if I hate doing the show?

But Trump played the What If Game instead:

- What if the show is a success?

- What if the show helps improve my brand?

- What if I love doing the show?

- What if it helps me make more money?

- What if it helps me find apprentices who are outstanding and can add value to my business?

- What if millions of people around the world fall in love with me and my Trump organization?

The What If Game stops negativity in its tracks and replaces it with positivity. It defuses all of the fears, doubts and uncertainties we all face when we pursue something new or worthwhile. It immediately changes the way we think. It gives us courage to move forward. The next time you are faced with a difficult decision, play the What If game. Don't give in to those demon voices. What if the demon voices are just wrong?

13. *Script Your Life* - Self-made millionaires do not stumble into success. They are not passive beneficiaries of some incredible stroke of good luck. The journey towards success always starts with a vision. A vision of the person you want to be and the life you want to have for yourself and their family. Sixty one percent of the self-made millionaires in my study engaged in something I call Dream-Setting. Dream-Setting involves

scripting your ideal, future life. In this process, you define your future life, the future you, by imagining all of your dreams coming true and then put it to paper in 500 - 1,000 words. This is the Future Letter strategy we covered previously. The Future Letter toggles on the Reticular Activating System (RAS) as well as the hippocampus. Once you turn on the RAS and the hippocampus, they go to work, behind the scenes, searching for ways to attract what you desire in your new, future life. They are like drones, programmed to find a target. In this case, the target is anything that will help you realize your dream. Your senses are programmed by the RAS to pick up any input from the outside world that will get you to your final destination. This data is then filtered through the hippocampus, which decides if this information will help you in achieving goals or realizing a dream. In a real sense, when the RAS is turned on, it allows you to see for the first time. Your eyes open up to opportunities that were always there, but that were previously invisible to you.

14. *Pursue Your Passion* - One of the common threads among all of the self-made millionaires in my study was a passion for what they did for a living. They were among the fortunate few who found their calling in life. Every wealthy entrepreneur in my study who realized incredible wealth had passion. Passion changes your beliefs about yourself. It infuses you with energy,

persistence, focus and patience. Each one of the wealthy entrepreneurs in my study had an intense desire to realize their dreams. They had a never ending focus on achieving their dream. They did not let obstacles get in their way. They believed in themselves. Their passion made miracles happen. These self-made millionaires all had six common traits: passion, persistence, focus, patience, a hard work ethic and a desire to learn. What's even more interesting is that, according to these wealthy individuals, they never knew they possessed those traits until they decided to pursue a dream. Pursuing that dream set in motion all of the other success traits. Passion has a domino effect on other success traits, bringing them to life. Passion trumps education. Passion trumps intelligence. Passion trumps working capital. Passion trumps skills and years of technical proficiency. Passion trumps any advantage, those who lack passion, might have in life. Those few who find passion in something, simply blow the doors off those who lack passion. It is not even a competition. Passion occurs when you find your main purpose in life. Having a main purpose is the key. It is the magic, secret ingredient to success because it makes passion possible. When you find your main purpose in life, you know it. It's not something you ponder. It hits you over the head like a hammer. You never wonder if you've found your main purpose in life. If you have any doubt, rest assured you haven't found your purpose in life. When you are following your main purpose in life you become a slave to it. The passion it creates becomes all consuming. But how do you find your main purpose in life? Believe it or not, finding your main purpose in life is within your control. Here's the process:

- Take out a sheet of paper and draw five columns.

- In the first column, make a list of everything you can ever remember that made you happy in life. Hopefully, this will be a long list.

- Now highlight those items on your list which involve a skill.

- In the second column, assign a job-type designation to each of the highlighted items.

- In the third column, rank each of the highlighted items in terms of happiness with number one being the greatest happiness and number two the next greatest happiness and so on.

- In the fourth column, rank each of the highlighted items in terms of income potential with number one being the highest income and number two being the next highest and so on.

- In the fifth column, total columns three and four. The lowest scores represent your main purpose in life.

Here is an example:

MAIN PURPOSE

DESCRIPTION	JOB CATEGORIES	HAPPY	$	TOTAL
WHEN I RAN FOR CAMPAIGN FOR CLASS PRESIDENT	POLITICIAN, CAMPAIGN MANAGER, PROFESSIONAL SPEAKER	1	3	4
WHEN I ORGANIZED THE SKY TRIP FOR OUR HIGH SCHOOL CLASS	EVENT PALNNING	2	2	4
WHEN I COACHED BASKETBALL PART-TIME IN COLLEGE	COACHING BASKETBALL	3	4	7
WHEN I WORKED PART-TIME IN COLLEGE SELLING CARS	NEW CAR SALESMAN, NEW CAR DEALERSHIP OWNER	6	1	7
WHEN I WROTE FOR THE SCHOOL NEWSPAPER	JOURNALIST, AUTHOR	4	5	9
ROTC	MILITARY CAREER	5	6	11

Once you've identified a number of possible activities that could become your main purpose in life, the next step is to engage in one of these activities for six months. If after six months you do not become obsessed with the activity, move on to the next activity. You know you've found your main purpose in life when you have no choice but to engage in the activity every day. You become obsessed. It is all you think about. Your main purpose is something that you just know you will do until the day you die. You will know that you found your main purpose in life when the activity does not feel like work. While engaged in pursuing your main purpose, time flies by. Before you know it, hours have passed. You will know you found your main purpose when you are infused with passion. Passion makes work fun. Passion gives you the energy, persistence and focus needed to overcome failures, mistakes and rejection. According to my research data, finding your main purpose in life creates the greatest long-term happiness and also results in the greatest accumulation of wealth. Those who pursue their own purpose in life love what they do for a living and are the happiest people. Making money becomes secondary to the joy you get in performing the activity that is your main purpose. Ironically, you will make more money than you ever imagined because, through repetitive practice, you will become expert in your craft. You will know you've found your main purpose in life when you are happy engaging in the activity and look forward to waking up in the morning to do the work that makes you happy.

15. *Persistence* - Self-made millionaires are persistent. They never quit on their dream. They would rather go down with the ship than quit. Twenty seven percent of the self-made millionaires in my study failed at least once in business. And then they picked themselves up and went on to try again. They persisted. Persistence requires doing certain things every day that move you forward in achieving your goals or life dream. Persistence makes you unstoppable. No obstacle, mistake or momentary failure will stop you from moving forward. You learn to pivot and change course, growing in the process. Persistence allows

you to learn what doesn't work and continuously experiment, until you find what does work. Persistence is the single greatest contributor to creating good luck. Those who persist, eventually get lucky. Some unintended consequence emerges. Some unexpected, unanticipated event happens to those who persist. Sometimes, those closest to you will urge you on and encourage you. But more often, those closest to you, those directly impacted by the obstacles, mistakes and failures that are part of the success journey, will try to stop you from persisting. It takes almost superhuman effort to achieve success when there are so many forces aligned against you. That's what makes successful people so special and so rare. If you want to be successful in life, you must persist in the face of seemingly unending adversity. Successful people are successful because they never ever quit!

16. *Don't Follow the Herd* - What do Facebook and Google have in common? The answer is The Herd Doctrine. Human beings have a herd mindset that is simply overpowering. It's what drives teens to engage in certain peer-driven behavior. It's also what made Facebook and Google possible. People simply want to blend in; they want to be part of the herd. We are all hardwired that way, genetically. It's a byproduct of the evolution of the human genome. During the early part of our human existence, we quickly discovered that when we were part of a herd, we were safe from predators. The Herd Doctrine ensured the very survival of

our species. We so desire to blend in, to acclimate to society, to be a part of the herd, that we will do almost anything to avoid standing out in a crowd. It's not theory. It's science (*http://www.nature.com/ srep/2013/131009/srep02905/full/srep02905.html*). Many years ago, Candid Camera decided to test this science in their famous Elevator Prank (*http:// www.maniacworld.com/peer-pressure-on-the-elevator.html*). In this skit, an innocent bystander is followed onto an elevator by a group of Candid Camera pranksters. Once the elevator starts moving, the pranksters all turn around, facing the opposite side of the elevator. The innocent bystander is clearly agitated by this. After a few moments the innocent bystander turns in the same direction of the pranksters. The pranksters then turn around once again and the innocent bystander does the same thing. They repeat this prank with many other innocent bystanders, and the result is always the same: the innocent bystander eventually follows the herd. As funny as that Candid Camera prank is, it highlights the lengths people will go to be part of the herd. If you are pursuing success, what you're really trying to do is create or grow your own herd and then get other individuals to join your new herd. There are two parts to the Herd Doctrine.

Part One – You must separate yourself from the herd - Failure to separate yourself from the herd is why most people never achieve success. The herd stops them in their tracks. The moment anyone in your herd gets wind that you are pursuing some big goal, life dream or purpose, they pounce on you. You are bombarded with all sorts of negativity. "What happens if you fail?" "Maybe it's too risky." "The odds of success are stacked against you." "You're not smart enough." "Where will you get the money?" It takes super human effort to persist in the face of such criticism. Most don't. They surrender to the herd.

Part Two – You must create your own herd and get others to join it - Successful people succeed because they are able to create their own new herd and then draw the attention of others, pulling them into their own new herd. Those who are enormously successful are able to get other herds to move to their product or service. When this happens it is as if these new herd creators realize overnight successes, even though it likely took them many years for the other herds to join their new herd. When you succeed in getting others to move to your new herd, you win. For example, when the Facebook herd was formed, a small number of individuals began joining the Facebook herd. Soon, word got out and more joined. Eventually millions who felt left out of the herd began quickly jumping on the Facebook herd bandwagon. That herd now has now grown to over a billion members. The founders of Google did exactly the same thing. They were able to move millions from other herds such as Yahoo and AOL to their new herd. Millionaires have big herds, deca-millionaires have bigger herds and billionaires have huge herds. The bigger your herd, the more successful you will be.

Understanding the Herd Doctrine is critical to success in life. You want to separate yourself from the herd, create your own herd and then get others to join it. In the beginning, it's a lonely journey. It takes time to get others to notice you. But if you have a good product or service and are persistent, your herd will grow and you will reap enormous rewards. Getting others to join their own new herd, is what millionaires and billionaires do. Successful people are actually herd creators and herd movers.

17. *Good Etiquette* - You have to know how to act and how to do certain things when you're around people. Self-made millionaires have mastered certain rules of etiquette that help them in social settings. Here are a few of the etiquette principles you have to master if you want to be a success:

- *Thank You Cards* - Saying thank you is a reflection of your character. When someone sends you a gift, send them a thank you card. Don't Facebook them, Tweet them, Instagram them. Send a thank you card. When should you send a thank you card to someone? When someone remembers your birthday. When someone acknowledges an important life event, such as a death in the family, birth, wedding, engagement, etc. When someone refers a customer or client to you, send them a thank you card. When someone does you or a direct family member a favor, send them a thank you card. After paying a friend or family member back who has lent you money, send a card. When someone acknowledges an accomplishment or achievement, send a card. When someone does anything good for you or a direct family member, they deserve a thank you card. When someone opens the door to an important contact for any reason or promotes anything that is important to you or a direct family member, send them a thank you card.

- *Properly Communicate* - Look everyone in the eye for no more than 5 seconds at a time, then divert your glance for another 5 seconds. Practice will turn this into a habit. Not every thought that comes into your head should come out of your mouth. Vet your thoughts. Speaking your mind does not mean sharing every thought. Some thoughts are not appropriate and could cause irreparable damage to your relationships. Never criticize, condemn or complain about anyone to anyone else. It's a giant red flag. People will assume that you are bad mouthing them and will avoid you. Never gossip. Most gossip is bad, negative and damages relationships. Gather as much information about your relationships as you can. At a minimum, gather the following information: birthdays, hobbies, interests, schools attended, where they grew up, current family background (married? kids?), where they live, dreams or goals they are pursuing. The more you know about your relationships, the more ammunition you'll have in your arsenal to help you in communicating with them. Make Hello Calls, Happy Birthday Calls and Life Event Calls.

- *Eating Etiquette* - Believe it or not, most people don't know how to eat. Many grow up eating while they watch T.V. or sitting at a table in a fast food restaurant. In the adult world of the high achievers, you need to know how to eat at social settings. Here's what you need to know: As soon as you sit in your chair, take the napkin off the table and drape it over your lap. Never begin eating until everyone has their meal. Never chew with your mouth opened. Never talk while you're chewing your food. Never dip any food you're eating into a sauce everyone is using. Don't wolf down your food. Eat at the same pace as everyone else at the table. Never hold a spoon, fork or knife with your fist. Outside fork is for salads, inside fork for the meal. Never make gestures while your utensils are in your hands. Never reach for anything like salt and pepper. Always ask someone to pass things like that. Don't slouch at the table. Sit straight up. After the meal, excuse yourself and go to the bathroom and make sure you don't have any food in your teeth. Carry a toothpick or something similar in your wallet or purse wherever you go.

- **Dress Etiquette** - You have to learn how to dress in life. There's a certain way to dress for work and job interviews. You're going to go to all sorts of social events: weddings, formal dinners, informal dinner parties, engagement parties, funerals, birthday parties, picnics, etc. You need to know how to dress. Here's a basic rundown:

  ➤ Work and Job Interviews – Some professions have special purpose clothing like construction, roadwork, electricians, etc. If you work in an office, dress like your boss or your boss's boss. In some offices its business casual. In others it's a suit and tie for men. For woman, its slacks, or skirts with open collars, heels or no heels are ok.

  ➤ Weddings, Wakes, Funerals – In most cases this will be suit and tie for men. For women it's the same as work clothes but many women like to wear more formal gowns or a more stylish cocktail dress, usually worn with heels. Some cultures have special dress codes you need to be aware of.

  ➤ Formals – Formals are black tie optional, black tie or white tie for men. Black tie optional means a tuxedo or a dark suit, tie or black bow tie and dark shoes. Black tie means black tuxedo, dark shoes. White tie means black tailcoat, white wing-collar shirt, white bow tie, black shoes for men. For women, formal means a long formal gown, short cocktail dress or dressy long skirt and top, usually worn with heels. White ties are typically very rare.

- *Introduce Yourself Properly* - In life you will be forced into situations where you will meet new people. This is an opportunity to develop valuable relationships. Some may be your next employer, future spouse, next best friend, future co-worker, investor or future business partner. There are a few basic rules in making introductions: Smile. Firm handshake. Make eye contact. In one sentence, explain who you are, why you're there and who you know at the event. Ask questions about the person you are introducing yourself to.

- *Basic Manners You Must Have* - There are some fundamental manners you will need in order to make yourself respectable in front of others: Say please and thank you. Don't interrupt someone while they are talking. Don't roll your eyes when someone says something you disagree with. Don't look away when someone is talking to you. Never check your cell phone when talking to someone. Stay positive and keep criticisms and negative comments to yourself. Compliment, compliment, compliment. Thank those hosting an event, dinner, etc. Never curse or use inappropriate language during social events. Never be rude

18. *Mentor Others* - We talked about the importance

of finding a mentor but I found in my research there is another mentoring Rich Habit that is almost as important and that is mentoring others. Mentoring other individuals makes you more expert at what you do because it forces you to teach what you've learned. Teaching is always the best way to learn anything. Mentoring others also pulls those you mentor into your herd and creates a devoted following that will pay dividends for the rest of your life.

19. ***Seek Out Cheerleaders and Avoid Booleaders*** - Negative, destructive criticism will derail you from pursuing success. As Charles Schwab, former President of Carnegie Steel, said so many years ago: "I have yet to find the man, however exalted his station, who did not do better work and put forth greater effort under a spirit of approval than under a spirit of criticism." Don't get me wrong, criticism is necessary for success. You need feedback from others. But all too often that feedback is mired in negative, destructive criticism that lacks any real specific constructive advice. "The reason you're not selling more is your product is terrible." "You're bossy, arrogant, pompous, or (fill in the blank)." You're failing because you're bad at what you do." "You're doing it all wrong or you need to change what you're doing." While most of this may be true, it lacks any constructive, specific feedback. You're wasting your time listening to it. Most criticism you will receive, is unfortunately going to be this negative,

generalized destructive type of criticism and not the positive, specific, constructive type you need. These Booleaders offer only negative criticism because they, themselves, have little to no idea how to help you. They've never succeeded in doing what you're doing, so their advice must be general and lack any specific, constructive feedback. This type of negative, destructive criticism only brings you down; it deflates you, slowing you down or stopping you on your path to success. When you are pursuing a dream, big goal or your purpose in life, you absolutely must seek out only those who offer positive, specific, constructive criticism. You need to seek out Cheerleaders and not Booleaders. Cheerleaders offer constructive feedback that will help you succeed. Their criticism has tremendous value because they know what they are talking about. Their knowledge is valuable because they have a track record of success in doing what you are attempting to do. They may also have a track record of helping others like you succeed. They have gravitas by virtue of their previous success. If you want to succeed in realizing your dream, you must surround yourself with Cheerleaders and avoid Booleaders.

20. *Believe* - Our beliefs can either create wealth or create poverty. If you believe you are smart, you are right. If you believe you are dumb, you are right. If you believe life is an oyster, you are right. If you believe life is a struggle, you are right. What we believe determines who we become in

life. Your beliefs are programming you picked up in life. Much of it was created in your youth, influenced by your parents, siblings and your environment. These programmed beliefs we acquire in childhood, follow us into adulthood. Some beliefs are positive and others negative, limiting beliefs. The positive beliefs enable us to achieve. Limiting beliefs hold us back, preventing us from realizing our full potential. Beliefs are stored in our conscious and subconscious mind. They are scattered about in the limbic system, the cerebral cortex, our prefrontal cortex and in many of the 100 billion neurons that make up the brain. Beliefs represent mini computer programs, which direct your behavior, choices and decisions in life. If you want to change your circumstances in life, you must change your beliefs. You need to adopt positive beliefs and erase negative, limiting beliefs. Here are some strategies to help you do that:

Future Letter Strategy

We already went over this strategy in detail but just to recap: The Future Year Letter strategy asks you to go out into your future and write a letter to yourself about how amazing your life is. You're basically creating a blueprint of you ideal, perfect life. You describe: where are you live, what cool stuff you own, vacations you go on, the amazing work you do that you love, etc.

Obituary Strategy

We went over this one previously but just to remind you the Obituary Strategy asks you to write a few words about the amazing life you lived. You include in it all of your amazing accomplishments and successes. You want to paint a picture with words of a life that leaves you awe struck.

List Your Wishes and Dreams

I'll cover this in much more detail later in the book but let me give you a little preview here. Once you have completed your Future Letter and Obituary you then list every wish or dream you find in them. Then reduce your list to the top ten wishes and dreams you find. This list will be your springboard for creating goals around those wishes and dreams.

Create Goals around Your Wishes and Dreams

Once again, I cover this in more detail in the Dream-Setting and Goal-Setting section later in the book. The fundamental principle here is to build individual goals around each of your wishes and dreams and then to tackle each goal, one at a time.

21. *Help Others Succeed* - Helping other success-minded people move forward in achieving their goals and dreams, helps you succeed. It's the "birds of a feather flock together" metaphor. The more success-minded people you help, in achieving their goals and realizing their dreams, the more

devotees you add to your life. No one realizes
success without a team of people behind them.
Successful people become successful because
they are able to create a valuable support team
of other success-minded people. The best way to
create your team is to offer help to other success-
minded people first. But just don't give help to
anyone. There's a reason I am using the phrase
"success-minded people." You want to focus on
helping only those who are pursuing success, are
optimistic, goal oriented, positive and uplifting.
This is an important point because most people
are not optimistic, goal oriented, positive, uplifting
people. Only about 5% will meet this criteria. So
you need to be very selective and take your time
selecting who to help.

22. *Make Thinking a Daily Habit*

*"Five percent of the people think; ten percent of the
people think they think; and the other eighty-five
percent would rather die than think."*
                                    — *Thomas Edison*

One of the things that stood out from my Rich
Habits Study was how important thinking was
to self-made millionaires. I tracked ten different
types of thinking habits these millionaires engaged
in frequently, if not daily. From my research, it was
so evident that thinking was key to their success,
that I decided it needed to become one of the ten
Keystone Rich Habits.

When self-millionaires think, they often do so in

isolation, closed off from the world. Most engaged in their daily thinking habits in the morning, some during their commute in their car, others in the shower, and still others at night. Morning seemed to be the most dominant time frame, however. Typically, immediately upon waking, these self-made millionaires would find a quite space and think. How long? It ranged from fifteen minutes to thirty minutes. What did they think about? Well, they thought about a lot of things and when they thought, they thought in a way that most would call brainstorming. They spent time every day brainstorming with themselves about numerous things. I was able to boil down those brainstorming sessions into ten core Rich Thinking Habit categories. Here they are:

i. *Career* – Some of the questions they asked themselves included: What can I do to make more money? How can I increase my value to my clients, customers or my employer? What do I need to do in order to gain more expertise? What additional skills do I need? What things should I be reading more about? Do I like what I do? What do I love to do? Can I make money doing what I love to do? Should I change careers? Should I work more hours? Should I work less hours? Do I work hard enough? Am I lazy? What am I really good at? What am I really bad at? Does my job make me happy?

ii. *Finances* – Do I spend too much money? Am

I saving enough money? Will I have enough to retire on? How much do I need to retire on? Do I have enough set aside for college for my kids? How much do I actually spend each month? Should I create a budget? Should I revise my budget? Am I doing a good job investing our money? Is my spouse doing a good job investing our money? Am I paying too much in taxes? Do I have enough life insurance? Should I set up a trust for my kids?

iii. *Family* – Do I spend enough time with my family? Can I work less and spend more time with my family? Are we spoiling our kids? Are we too hard on our kids? Can I get away for a vacation this year? Are we doing enough to help our kids succeed? How can I improve my relationship with my spouse, my kids?

iv. *Friends* – Do I have as many friends as I should? Do I spend enough time with the friends I have? Why don't I have many friends? How can I make more friends? Is my work interfering too much with my social life? Do I call my friends enough? How often should I stay in touch with my friends? Who haven't I spoken with in a while? Do I have good friends? How can I end my friendship with so and so? Should I help my friends financially?

v. *Business Relationships* – What can I do to improve my business relationships? Am I staying in touch enough with my key customers, clients? How can I develop a business relationship with so and so? Which business relationships should I spend more time on and which ones should I pull away from? Do my customers, clients like me? Do they think I do a good job?

vi. *Health* – Am I exercising enough? Should I lose more weight? Do I eat too much? Am I eating healthy? Should I get a physical? Should I take vitamins/supplements? I need to get a colonoscopy. Are my arteries clogged? Do I get enough sleep? Do I drink too much? I have to stop smoking. I have to cut back on junk food. I need to eat more vegetables.

vii. *Dream-Setting and Goal-Setting* – Most of the brainstorming involved their personal, financial, family and career dreams and goals. Dreams of retiring on a beach, buying a boat, expanding their business, buying vacation homes, etc.

viii. *Problems* – Here they brainstormed primarily about finding solutions to those problems that were causing them the most stress at the moment. Most were immediate problems related to their jobs and their family. Some were longer term and related to preempting future potential problems they were anticipating down the road most often related to their careers.

ix. *Charity* – What other charities can I get

involved in? Am I doing enough for my church, business group, synagogue, etc.? How can I best help my community? What can I do to help my grammar school, high school, college, etc.? Should I start a scholarship? Should I contribute more money to my school, church, etc.? Who can I help?

x. *Happiness* – Am I happy? What is causing me to be unhappy? How can I eliminate those things that are making me unhappy? Is my spouse happy? Are my kids happy? Are my employees or staff happy? How can I make myself happier? What is happiness? Will I ever be happy? What's making me so happy?

That's a lot of thinking, I know. There are a lot of days in the year, however, to brainstorm. You just need to make it a daily habit. Eventually, over time, you will come up with solutions to your most pressing problems. You will gain insight into what makes you tick. Daily thinking will help you find some meaning to your life. Making a daily habit of thinking is what self-made millionaires do. It's an important piece of the success puzzle. Understanding why they do it is less important than understanding that they do do it. Every day.

23. *Ask For What You Want* – Fear holds most back from asking for something from someone else. Actually two types of fear: fear of being rejected and fear of obligation. Self-made millionaires overcome these fears and make a habit of asking

everyone they can for help. A few of the millionaires in my study said they figured out some people really do want to help and that asking for help was a numbers game. Some will say no, but some will say yes and offer to help. I personally struggle with this Rich Habit, quite frankly. Let me tell you how I overcame these fears recently. SUCCESS Magazine was profiling me in their November 2014 edition and it dawned on me that I might not have enough money to meet the demand for books (I was self-published). It took me three weeks to muster the courage to make my first phone call to a millionaire to help fund the book sales. For three weeks I dragged my feet. I was consumed with fear and doubts. But I knew from my research that self-made millionaires, despite their fears, ask for help. So I did. Much to my surprise the first millionaire I called was willing to front me $150,000 to meet the demand. It's the fear of rejection and the fear of obligation that prevents us from asking for what we want. You have to get over those fears and keep asking until someone says yes, if you want to be successful in life. As the Bible says, "ask and you shall receive." There's a lot of wisdom in that saying.

24. *Avoid Negativity* – While we already discussed the need to avoid negative, toxic people, there is a broader need to avoid any and all negative influences. These often come from people but they may also come from the media: T.V., Internet sites, newspapers, radio, magazines, books and podcasts. Don't spend too much time reading, listening to or

watching news. News is constructed to be negative because negativity taps into our natural born fears. While you need to stay current with events, it is a bad habit to immerse yourself in news. Reading the news will shift your thinking from positive to negative almost immediately. It causes anxiety, stress, sadness and in some cases, depression.

25. *Take Calculated Risks* – Self-made millionaires, while not reckless, are nonetheless able to overcome their fear of failure and take calculated risks. These risks are not without cost. During the journey towards wealth accumulation, many lose money. All of the self-made millionaires in my study invested their own money and most took on debt from banks, family and friends in pursuit of their dream. Twenty seven percent actually experienced failure in their ventures and had to start all over. The important point here is that they did start over. They failed, made mistakes and used the lessons they learned from these failures and mistakes to help them to ultimately succeed. The pursuit of wealth requires that you take risks. Most don't, and that's why most are not wealthy.

26. *Seek Feedback* – Fear of criticism is the reason we do not seek feedback from others. But feedback is essential to learning what is working and what isn't working. Feedback helps you understand if you are on the right track. Seeking criticism, good or bad, is a crucial element for learning and growth. It also allows you to change course. The most successful self-made millionaires piloted

new ventures before they dove in with both feet. Piloting a new initiative, either by engaging in it on a part-time basis or on a limited basis, provides valuable information that you can use when you decide to go for it; to devote all of your resources and time to the venture. Feedback provides you with the information you will need in order to succeed in any venture.

Poor Habits – Habits That Hold You Back From Success

Poor Habits will make you unhappy, unhealthy and negative. They will cause depression, relationship problems and financial struggles. All habits cause outcomes and Poor Habits create negative outcomes in your life. In order to transform your life, you need to adopt good habits and eliminate bad habits. The Rich Habits are unique good habits because they were constructed to be Keystone Habits. What makes Keystone Habits unique is their ability to stop poor habits in their tracks. Adopting one Rich Habit has the effect of eliminating many Poor Habits. That's why the Rich Habits are so powerful. Each one you adopt is like a double or triple in baseball. It moves you towards success much faster. But in order to know which Rich Habits to adopt, you need to first identify your own individual Poor Habits. Below is a top ten list of some of the worst Poor Habits that are dragging you down and creating a life of misery:

1. *Gambling* - Gambling is the pursuit of success

without the sweat. There is no such thing as getting rich quick. Financial success takes time, takes effort and requires relentless effort. Those who gamble are deluded into thinking there is a short cut to success. Fifty two percent of the poor in my study gambled on sports at least once a week and 77% played the lottery every week. Self-made millionaires don't gamble. In my study, 84% did not bet on sports and 94% did not play the lottery. The odds of gambling and winning are infinitesimal. Self-made millionaires don't pursue any get rich quick schemes. Instead, they make a habit of pursuing their dreams and their goals.

2. ***Drinking Too Much Alcohol*** – Fifty four percent of the poor in my study drank more than two glasses of beer, wine or alcohol each day. Eighty four percent of the self-made millionaires in my study drank less than that. Worse, 60% of the poor in my study got drunk at least once a month. Drinking clogs neuro-receptors on brain cells, causing them to misfire, or not fire at all. This affects your memory and ability to think clearly. Drinking also adds significant calories to your daily diet and, over time, will cause you to become overweight or obese.

3. ***Watching Too Much T.V.*** – Seventy seven percent of the poor in my study watched more than an hour of T.V. every day. Sixty seven percent of the self-made millionaires in my study watched less than an hour of T.V. every day. Watching T.V. is a time waster and the inactivity associated with it is

bad for your health. Facebook, Twitter, You Tube and other newly emerging social media platforms are replacing T.V. watching habits, but they are Poor Habits just the same. Making productive use of time is a hallmark of self-made millionaires. Wasting time is a hallmark of poor people.

4. *Negative Mindset* – Seventy eight percent of the poor in my study had a negative mindset. Fifty four percent of the self-made millionaires in my study had a positive mindset. You cannot succeed in life if you have the Poor Habit of thinking negative thoughts. When you see everything in your life in a negative way, you will attract more negativity into your life. Once again, this is the brain's Reticular Activating System (RAS) and hippocampus at work seeking to provide you with a reality that is consistent with your thoughts. Thinking "I don't make enough money" is a directive to the RAS and hippocampus to go to work behind the scene, diligently nudging you to do things that will make sure you don't have enough money. "I have bad luck" puts them to work seeking bad luck. "Nothing ever goes my way" will put the RAS and hippocampus to work 24/7 making sure everything goes wrong in your life. "People are mean" makes them look for mean people for you to associate with. "I don't trust anyone" is a directive to these two parts of the brain to find untrustworthy people. "Rich people are evil" virtually ensures that you will never become rich. "I'm poor because I was born poor" is a negative limiting belief that programs the RAS

and hippocampus to make sure you stay poor. "I can't afford (fill in the blank)." "I'm not smart or educated enough." "It's not my fault I'm poor." "The rich or the government is causing my poverty." "Life is a struggle." I can go on and on. You get the point. When you allow negativity to rule your thoughts, you are programming your brain for failure. You'll have no chance in life at breaking out of your current financial or life circumstances. These negative thoughts will become beliefs that act like computer programs. Worse, if you have children, they will adopt your negative thinking and struggle in life as adults. This is why the saying "the poor get poorer" has so much truth to it.

5. *You Don't Read* – Ninety two percent of the poor in my study did not read to learn. Seventy nine percent of those who did read, read for entertainment. Success requires growth. That growth comes from reading and educating yourself on a daily basis. If you want to succeed in life you must engage in daily self-improvement reading.

6. *You Have Toxic Relationships* - Only 4% of the poor in my study associated with success-minded individuals. Ninety six percent associated with negative, toxic individuals. You are only going to succeed in life if you surround yourself with the right type of people.

7. *One Stream of Income* - Poor people have one income stream. Their eggs are all in one basket. Typically, that one stream of income is a job. If they

lose that job, they lose their only source of income.

8. *No Life Plan* – Ninety five percent of the poor in my study had no life plan. They never took the time to develop a blueprint for their future life. Success is a process. It starts by developing a script of the life you desire. This script becomes your blueprint for success. It helps you define your long-term goals. Without a blueprint, without long-term goals, we are like leaves on a fall day, floating in the air aimlessly.

9. *You Spend More Than You Make* – Ninety five percent of the poor in my study did not save and most accumulated debt to subsidize their standard of living. Consequently, they have no money for retirement, college for their kids or for pursuing opportunities that present themselves. Eighty eight percent owed more than $5,000 in credit card debt. Not saving and spending more than you make creates long-term poverty, with no hope of escape.

10. *Poor Health Habits* – Seventy seven percent of the poor in my study did not exercise. Ninety seven percent ate more than 300 junk food calories each day. Sixty nine percent frequented fast food restaurants three or more times a week. Eighty six percent did not floss daily. Sixty nine percent ate candy more than twice a week. Fifty three percent got less than seven hours of sleep each day. Sixty six percent were thirty pounds or more overweight. Poor health habits create Detrimental Luck. This

is a type of bad luck that is the byproduct of poor habits, poor behavior and bad decision making. Detrimental Luck caused by poor health habits can result in diabetes, heart disease, cancer, high blood pressure or any number of diseases or disabilities.

Do any of these Poor Habits look familiar? Not to worry. I will show you exactly how to eliminate your Poor Habits and create your own personalized daily Rich Habits. Each individual has their own specific Poor Habits that are holding them back. The key to transforming your life is to eliminate old Poor Habits and replace them with new Rich Habits. I will show you exactly how to do this.

THE HABITS SEESAW

Now that we've had a chance to better understand the difference between Rich Habits and Poor Habits, it's time to talk about the Habit Seesaw. Visualize a seesaw. Now imagine on one side of your seesaw are all of your Rich Habits and on the other side are all of your Poor Habits. If you want to be wealthy, more than 50% of all of your daily habits must be Rich Habits. If you are poor, this is because more than 50% of all of your daily habits are Poor Habits. If you are stuck in the middle-class, this means that you have a 50/50 split of Rich Habits and Poor Habits on your Habit Seesaw.

Getting your seesaw to tip in the right direction, towards wealth accumulation, may be as simple as changing a few daily habits. For example, if you are in the middle-class and you want to become wealthy you only need to add two or three Rich Habits or you only need to eliminate two or three Poor Habits. If you are poor and you want to become wealthy you will have to add a few more Rich Habits and/or eliminate a few more Poor Habits.

The point I want to make here is that the difference

between being rich or poor is not much. It requires only a few minor changes to your daily routine. As mentioned previously, 40% of all of our daily activities are habits. This means 40% of the time we are all on auto pilot. Forty percent of the time we don't even think about what we are doing during the day. We are all in zombie mode 40% of the time. Now, if you have good daily habits, then this is a good thing. But if you have bad daily habits, then this is a bad thing. Without much thought you are either on the path to creating wealth or poverty. Daily habits are responsible for your wealth, poverty, happiness and unhappiness. The key is to get that Habit Seesaw tipping in the right direction and I will show you exactly how to make that happen.

PART III
CREATING
HABITS AROUND
DREAMS AND
GOALS

DREAM-SETTING

Self-made millionaires do not rely on fate, random good luck, God or the benevolence of others to secure the life they desire. They take action. Successful people shape the course of their own lives. There are a number of strategies they use to create a blueprint for the life they desire: Dream-Setting, Goal-Setting and Building Habits Around Individual Goals.

Dream-Setting is the act of clearly defining a dream. Dreams represent a vision of some future, ideal state or reality. It's a two-step process:

Step One – Ask yourself what you want your ideal life to be ten, fifteen or twenty years out. Then write down every detail of your ideal future life. Be very specific in the details: the income you earn, the house you live in, the boat you own, the car you drive, the money you've accumulated, etc. This is the Future Letter strategy that I referred to previously.

Step Two – Using this detailed description of your ideal future life, make a bullet point list of each one of the details that represent your ideal life. These would be the income you earn, the house you live in, the boat your own, etc. These details represent your wishes or dreams.

In my research, I uncovered seven strategies, I call the Future Mirror Strategies, that successful people use to create a blueprint for their perfect, ideal life. Each one of these strategies represents a future, ideal state. Let me share them with you:

1. *Your Soul Mate* – Who do you want to spend the rest of your life with? What kind of person is your soul mate? Are they upbeat, enthusiastic, happy and anxious to succeed in life? In 100 words or less, paint a picture with words, exactly who and what this person is. What they look like; what they do for a living; who their friends are; their type of personality? Describe in intricate detail everything about this person who you will share the rest of your life with.

2. *Your Career* – What is your ideal job? How much money do you make? What type of people do you work with? What does your ideal work day look like? What exotic places does your ideal job take you? What skills do you acquire in your perfect career? Once again, try to keep it to 100 words.

3. *Your Health* – How much do you want to weigh? What shape are you in? What do you do to stay in shape? What types of food do you eat that keep you fit and trim? Once again, try to keep it to 100 words.

4. *Your Home* – What does your ideal home look like? Where do you live? How big is your home? How much money is it worth? How many rooms does it have? Describe those rooms. Describe your neighborhood. Leave nothing out. Again, keep to 100 words.

5. *Your Activities* – In your ideal life, what kind of extracurricular activities do you engage in every day, every weekend, on vacation, etc? These can be hobbies, side businesses or activities that you are passionate about. Again, keep to 100 words.

6. *Your Stuff* – What things do you own? What kind of toys do you have? What car do you drive? What does your watch look like? How about your clothes? How much money do you have? How do you invest your wealth? Again, 100 words is all you need.

7. *The Big Picture* – The final strategy requires that you pull it all together. In 1,000 words or less, script your ideal life. Spare no details. Identify the specific people, career, health, home, toys, money and goals achieved that you want as a part of your perfect life. This big picture will become the blueprint of your life. It gives you a clear picture of your destination.

After you have defined your "Big Picture" through this scripting process, the next step is to make a list of all of your dreams and wishes, by referring back to your "Big Picture" script of your ideal, future life. This dream/wish list will be the spring board for creating specific goals around each one of your dreams.

GOAL-SETTING

Only after you've defined your wishes or dreams, does the Goal-Setting process begin. This Goal-Setting process requires you to build goals around each one of your wishes or dreams. In order to build goals around each wish or dream you need to ask yourself two questions:

Question #1: What would I need to do, what activities would I need to engage in, in order for each wish or dream to come true?

Question #2: Can I perform those activities?

If the answer to Question #2 is yes, then those activities represent your goals. Goals are only goals when they involve physical action and you have the capability to successfully take action. For example, if your wish is to make $200,000, what would you need to do, in a given year, in order to make $200,000? What specific activities would you need to engage in successfully during a given year, in order to make $200,000? Make more telemarketing phone calls? Do more training? Get a specific license in your industry? Expand your product offering? Purchase more rental properties? Invest in more efficient equipment or technology? Then you must ask yourself if you have the capability to do these things. So you have the necessary knowledge and skills to take action? If you do, then each action you must take represents a goal. If you don't have the capability to act then you must develop that capability before you can even begin to pursue each individual goal.

Let me give you another example:

Let's say you're a salesman and you want to increase your income by $100,000 a year. That $100,000 is a dream. What do you need to do in order for that dream to come true? What action steps must you accomplish in order to realize that $50,000? Let's break it down:

- How much is an average sale? Answer - $5,000

- What is your commission on each sale? Answer - $500

- How many sales will it take to reach $50,000? Answer - 100

- How do you go about prospecting for sales? Answer - making phone calls is the best method

- How many phone calls does it take for you to set up one sales meeting? Answer - five phone calls

- How many meetings does it take to close one sale? Answer - four meetings

- How many meetings will it take to reach $50,000? Answer - 400 meetings

- How many phone calls will it take to get those 400 meetings - Answer - 2,000

- How many days do you work each year? Answer - 250

- How many phone calls will you need to make each day to get those 400 meetings, 100 sales and your additional $50,000? Answer - eight phone calls each day.

In order to make an additional $50,000 you will need to make eight phone calls each day – a daily habit. Can you make eight phone calls each day? If the answer is yes then this is your daily habit – making eight phone calls each day.

SUMMARY: BUILDING HABITS AROUND INDIVIDUAL GOALS

Essentially, there's a two-step process to building a house:

1. Draw up Blueprints
2. Construct the House

Seems pretty simple, doesn't it? Each component of your house must be defined in the blueprint and then built: the kitchen, bathrooms, family room, dining room, bedrooms, and anything else you want your house to have, are the components of your house.

Constructing an ideal, happy and successful life is no different. It's the same process. In the case of your ideal life, the components of your life's blueprint are all of the things that make a perfect life: the job you want to have, what you would love to do for a living, the place you want to live, the life partner you'd like to share your life with, the places you'd like to travel to, the wealth you'd like to accumulate, etc. These are known as dreams or wishes.

You start building your ideal life by defining all of your dreams and wishes which, when taken together, become the blueprint of your life.

Your goals are your construction team. You need to define all of the goals that will make all of your dreams and wishes become a reality. You design your goals around each dream or wish. One dream or wish could require the achievement of one, five or ten goals. The realization of each dream or wish happens when you accomplish all of the goals that are required in order for each specific dream or wish to be realized. It's just like building a house. The kitchen is similar to an individual dream. To complete your kitchen you must perform certain tasks. Each task is a goal and each goal needs to be competed in order to build your kitchen (realize your dream or wish). Then you move on to the bathrooms, family room, dining room, bedrooms and anything else that will be included in your house. Each specific component of your house is an individual dream or wish that requires the completion of certain tasks (goals). Similarly, constructing an ideal life requires the completion (realization) of each dream or wish, as if it were a kitchen or living room. When all of your dreams and wishes are completed (realized) your ideal life is fully constructed.

You can automatically process certain activities into your day that will allow you to achieve your individual goals. These daily activities are your habits. You need to build daily habits around each goal. Habits put you on autopilot. They take the struggle out of achieving your goals. Put each daily habit on your to-do list and track the completion of those habits. This is what successful people do. They automate success. And habits are how they automate success every day.

Let's summarize this Dream-Setting, Goal-Setting and Habits-Building process:

- Paint a picture with words of your ideal life.

- Define each dream or wish that must be realized in order to have your ideal future life.

- Establish specific goals around each one of your dreams or wishes.

- Build daily activities (habits) around each individual goal.

You then repeat this process for every other dream or wish.

PART IV
CHANGING
YOUR HABITS

INTRODUCTION

If you don't know what you're doing, changing just one habit is hard. Remember, the brain fights you when it comes to habit change. As a result, most newly formed habits fall apart after a few weeks. Also, when you end an old habit, after a few weeks the brain eventually forces you back into those old habits. Eventually, your motivation and willpower wears off or you become stressed and your old habits rear their heads. If you don't know the tricks to habit change you have to rely on something I call Extreme Disgust to force habit change. Extreme Disgust is hard to come by. It's essentially hitting rock bottom - you are simply fed up with your life circumstances and you are able to muster an unusually powerful type of willpower that enables you to change your habits. But, as I said, that's unusual. You don't want to have to wait until your life falls apart because of your habits. You don't want to wait to hit rock bottom.

After more than eleven years of studying the habits of over 350 wealthy and poor people, I uncovered certain principles on habit change that make the process infinitely easier. I created an easy to follow program that will give you the tools to change your habits in just twenty one days. That's why you bought this book. You want a simple, easy to follow habit change process in order to avoid getting to that rock bottom point in your life. In addition to this easy to follow process, I'm going to share with you the latest in habit change science that will enable you to trick you brain into changing your habits without putting up a fight. This is what you've been waiting for. The buildup is over. Now fasten your seat belts because your life is about to change in ways you could only have dreamed of. Let's get started.

HABIT AWARENESS

In order to change your habits, you need to first become aware of them. Awareness requires tracking all of your habits, from the moment you wake up, to the moment you go to sleep. Two days of tracking is all it takes. You want to do this during the workweek because most habits are triggered by the environment and during periods of stress. The workplace is the most common source of stress. Below is an example of a Habit Awareness Schedule:

HABIT AWARENESS SCHEDULE

1	Wake up at 8 am to begin my day
2	Have a cup of coffee with a buttered bagel
3	Smoke a cigarette with my coffee
4	Shower and get ready for work
5	Commute to work in my car. Smoke a cigarette during my commute
6	Listen to music or talk radio during my commute
7	Check email and voicemail first thing at work
8	Respond to emails and voicemail first thing at work
9	Work

10	Take break, gossip with collegues for 15 minutes
11	Respond to emails and phone calls as they come in during morning
12	Lunch with colleagues at a fast food restaurant
13	Gossip during lunch
14	Work in the afternoon
15	Respond to emails and phone calls as they come in during afternoon
16	Take break, gossip with collegues, and grab a smoke for 15 minutes
17	Leave work at 5 pm
18	Commute home and listen to talk shows, the news, or music
19	Eat dinner, have a few beers or some wine
20	Watch TV for three hours
21	Read science fiction book in bed for an hour or more
22	Fall asleep between 11 to 11:30 pm

Use the blank schedule below to track your habits and create your own Habit Awareness Schedule

HABIT AWARENESS SCHEDULE

1	
2	
3	
4	
5	
6	
7	
8	
9	
10	

11	
12	
13	
14	
15	
16	
17	
18	
19	
20	
21	
22	

HABIT GRADING

The next step in the habit change process is to grade the habits you currently have. Put a plus (+) next to good habits and a minus (–) next to bad habits. Here's an example:

HABIT GRADING SCHEDULE

1	Wake up at 8 am to begin my day	–
2	Have a cup of coffee with a buttered bagel	–
3	Smoke a cigarette with my coffee	–
4	Shower and get ready for work	
5	Commute to work in my car. Smoke a cigarette during my commute	–
6	Listen to music or talk radio during my commute	–
7	Check email and voicemail first thing at work	–
8	Respond to emails and voicemail first thing at work	–
9	Work	+
10	Take break, gossip with collegues for 15 minutes	–
11	Respond to emails and phone calls as they come in during morning	–

12	Lunch with colleagues at a fast food restaurant	–
13	Gossip during lunch	–
14	Work in the afternoon	+
15	Respond to emails and phone calls as they come in during afternoon	–
16	Take break, gossip with collegues and grab a smoke for 15 minutes	–
17	Leave work at 5 pm	–
18	Commute from work and listen to talk shows, news or music	–
19	Eat dinner, have a few beers or some wine	–
20	Watch TV for three hours	–
21	Read science fiction book in bed for an hour or more	–
22	Fall asleep between 11 to 11:30 pm	–

Now create your own Habit Grading Schedule using the Habits Awareness Schedule you just created:

HABIT GRADING SCHEDULE

		+ OR –
1		
2		
3		
4		
5		
6		
7		

8		
9		
10		
11		
12		
13		
14		
15		
16		
17		
18		
19		
20		
21		
22		

This Habit Grading Schedule is your springboard for changing your habits. Don't worry that most of your habits are bad habits. The purpose of this exercise is to become aware of your bad habits. Awareness comes first in the habit change process. When you know which habits are holding you back, you have the information you need to transform your life. Most people, unfortunately, skip this step entirely and jump right into adding new habits. Millions do this every year when they set New Year's resolutions. They never become aware of the existing habits they have, which are creating the foundation for the life they have. Habit change requires that you eliminate bad habits and then add new good habits. The goal is to tip your individual Habit Seesaw in the right direction. In order to do that, you need to become aware of the habits you currently have, and then identify them as good or bad.

RICH HABITS CHECKLIST –
PHASE ONE:
MORNING HABITS

Now that you have identified all of your good and bad habits, it's time to begin creating your own customized Rich Habits Checklist. This checklist will eventually become part of your new daily routine. Habit change is a process. It takes time. The best approach is to focus on changing a few simple habits first. Phase One in this process is to select some morning habits you would like to change over the next seven day period. Here is an example:

RICH HABITS CHECKLIST - PHASE ONE: MORNING

I woke at 6 am this morning
I read for learning for thirty minutes this morning
I exercised for thirty minutes this morning
I prepared my to-do list this morning
During my commute to work I listened to audio books or a podcast this morning

| I did not eat any junk food this morning |
| I did not repeatedly check my email this morning |
| I did 3 things this morning that were related to my personal goals |

Rich Habits Tips:

Forty four percent of the wealthy, successful people in my Rich Habits Study woke up 3 hours or more before their work day began. This morning time was earmarked for self-education reading, exercise and other activities such as pursuing a goal, pursuing a passion, planning their day, writing, working a side business they were passionate about, studying for night school, etc. Those early morning hours represent an investment you make in yourself, every day. Take some time to create your own Rich Habits Morning Checklist:

RICH HABITS CHECKLIST - PHASE ONE: MORNING

	SUN	MON	TUE	WED	THU	FRI	SAT

For the next seven days this becomes your own customized Rich Habits Morning Checklist. Each day, check off every new Rich Habit you follow. This checklist will help force accountability in following your new morning Rich Habits. After seven days, these habits will begin to take root, creating synapses inside your brain that grow stronger every time you repeat each new habit. If you are able to check off 30% or more of your new habits, pat yourself on the back. It's important to understand that just changing a handful of your daily habits will have a profound impact on your life.

RICH HABITS CHECKLIST – PHASE TWO: DAYTIME HABITS

After following your Rich Habits Morning Checklist for at least seven days, you are now ready to move on to the next phase, changing your daytime habits using the same Rich Habits chunking process. Here is an example:

RICH HABITS CHECKLIST - PHASE TWO: DAYTIME

I read for learning for thirty minutes during lunch or I worked on goal-related tasks during lunch
I did not gossip with fellow workers during lunch or in the afternoon
I did not eat any junk food at lunch or in the afternoon
I checked and responded to email/voicemail from 1 to 2 pm
During my commute from work I listened to audio books or a podcast
I drank a glass of water instead of coffee this afternoon
I made some hello calls, happy birthday calls, or life event calls this afternoon
I did two things this afternoon that were related to my personal goals

Rich Habits Tips:

Sixty three percent of the wealthy individuals in my study listened to audio books or podcasts during their commute to and from work. Ninety five percent of the poor individuals in my study listened to radio talk shows or music during their commute. Seventy nine percent of the wealthy individuals in my study did not smoke cigarettes, while 46% of the poor did. Gossip almost always is negative. Ninety four percent of the wealthy in my study did not engage in gossip, while 79% of the poor in my study engaged in gossip on a daily basis. Seventy percent of the wealthy in my study ate less than 300 junk food calories a day, while 97% of the poor in my study ate more than 300 junk calories a day. The wealthy in my study dedicated specific time slots for responding to email and voicemail. This allowed them to focus on being productive, helping them avoid distractions. The poor in my study responded to email and voicemail throughout the day.

Take some time to now create your own Rich Habits Daytime Checklist:

RICH HABITS CHECKLIST - PHASE TWO: DAYTIME

	SUN	MON	TUE	WED	THU	FRI	SAT

Once again, you want to devote at least seven days to following your new daytime habits. Continue to follow your morning habits while simultaneously working on incorporating these new daytime habits into your routine. You may want to consolidate both the new morning and daytime habits onto the following checklist.

RICH HABITS CHECKLIST - MORNING & DAYTIME

	SUN	MON	TUE	WED	THU	FRI	SAT

RICH HABITS CHECKLIST – PHASE THREE: NIGHT TIME HABITS

After another seven days, you are ready for Phase Three. In Phase Three you will be adding new nighttime habits to your daily routine. Once again, the springboard for creating your new nighttime habits will be the Habit Awareness Schedule you completed earlier. Here is an example:

RICH HABITS CHECKLIST - PHASE THREE: NIGHT TIME

I watched less than one hour of TV tonight
I spent less than one hour on recreational Internet tonight
I spent one hour or more pursuing a dream, goal, or developing a side business or marketable skill
I met with my networking group, nonprofit group, or business group tonight
I coached my son's sports team tonight
I did thirty minutes of self-education reading tonight
I got to bed no later than 10 pm tonight

Rich Habits Tips:

Sixty seven percent of the wealthy in my study watched less than 1 hour of T.V. each day while 77% of the poor in my study watched more than 1 hour of T.V. each day. Sixty three percent of the wealthy in my study spent less than 1 hour each day on recreational Internet use while 74% of the poor in my study spent more than 1 hour a day on the Internet recreationally, visiting sites like Facebook, YouTube or Twitter. Sixty two percent of the wealthy in my study devoted time every day pursuing some goal, verses only 6% of the poor. Getting at least seven to eight hours of sleep every night is critical for your health, particularly brain health. The wealthy in my study averaged about 7 1/2 hours of sleep a night, while the poor averaged less than seven hours.

Take some time to now create your own Rich Habits Daytime Checklist:

RICH HABITS CHECKLIST - PHASE THREE: NIGHT TIME

	SUN	MON	TUE	WED	THU	FRI	SAT

Once again, you want to devote at least seven days to following your new nighttime habits. Continue to follow your morning and daytime habits, while simultaneously working on incorporating these new nighttime habits into your routine.

RICH HABITS CHECKLIST – CONSOLIDATING YOUR NEW HABITS

You may want to consolidate all of your new habits on the following schedule:

RICH HABITS CHECKLIST - CONSOLIDATED

	SUN	MON	TUE	WED	THU	FRI	SAT

Once your Consolidated Rich Habits checklist is complete, use it every day to hold yourself accountable. Over time, your new Rich Habits will become automatic. They will not require any willpower or thought. These habits will create a foundation for success in your life. They will pay dividends that will dramatically improve your financial circumstances, make you more confident and automatically put you on a path towards success. They are an investment in you, in your growth and in your happiness. Think of your Rich Habits as snowflakes on a mountainside. Over time your Rich Habits, like snowflakes, will accumulate. You will not notice the accumulation from day to day, but at some point they will create an avalanche; an avalanche of success event. It might be a bonus, raise, promotion, better job, big customer or clients or simply better health.

SHORT CUTS TO
HABIT CHANGE

There are six powerful shortcuts to habit change that speed up the process: Habit Merging, Law of Association, Changes in Your Environment, Starting Small, Scheduling Your New Habits and Firewalling Your Bad Habits. Each one of these makes habit change easier, quicker and requires less willpower.

Habit Merging

Think of an existing habit (existing neural pathway) as a train on a track, except it's inside your brain. If you add your new habit to that same train, as if it were a new passenger, the brain won't put up a fight because you're not trying to take control of the train or the track. You're just taking a ride. When an old habit does not perceive a new habit as a threat, it does not wage war against the formation of the new habit.

Here's how it works: Let's say you want to add a new Rich Habit of reading thirty minutes every day for self-education and let's say you have an old habit of exercising aerobically on the stair master thirty minutes every day. If you were to put a book on the stair master and read that book while you're exercising, you will, almost immediately, form a new joint habit that sticks. The trigger for the habit will be the book on your stair master. Here's another example: If you have an old habit of drinking coffee every day and you want to add a new Rich Habit of drinking a glass of water every day, you will put your coffee cup on a water cooler or in your sink or in your refrigerator, next to the water bottle. When your brain tells you it's time to drink coffee, you will, initially, search for your coffee cup. That coffee cup will then become a trigger, reminding you to drink a cup of water. That new joint habit will only take a few days to stick.

Law of Association

Old habits can be triggered by the individuals you associate with. If you are trying to get rid of some old, bad habits you need to limit the time you spend associating with those individuals who act as a trigger for those bad habits and begin associating with individuals who possess the new good habits you are trying to adopt. You can find these new individuals in network groups, non-profit groups, trade groups or any group that is focused on pursuing similar goals. For example, if one of your new goals is to read more, you can join a reading group that meets periodically to discuss books the group reads. Another example would be finding individuals who run, jog or exercise and begin jogging, running or exercising with them. Once you open your eyes to habit change, you will begin to see that there are many individuals who have those same habits. They are all around you. You only begin to notice them after you make a decision to change your daily habits.

Changes in Your Environment

It is much easier to abandon old habits and form new habits when your environment changes. New home, new neighbors, new friends, new job, new colleagues, new cities, etc., all offer an opportunity to forge new habits. When your environment changes, you are forced to think your way through each day. Spoons, knives and forks are no longer where they used to be, so you have to think. Your commute to work is different, so you have to think. Your new responsibilities at work are different, so you have to think. Eventually your brain will force you to develop habits in your new environment in order to make the brain's job easier.

Start Small

It is far easier to change your habits if you start with small habits. Small habit change involves adding habits that require very little effort. Examples include drinking more water during the day, taking vitamin supplements or listening to audio books while you commute to work. Small habit change also includes cutting back on existing bad habits. Examples include reducing the number of cigarettes you smoke, reduce T.V. watching by thirty minutes each day or reducing Facebook or Internet use to less than an hour a day. The smaller, easier the habit change, the higher the probability that it will stick. Small habit change gives you momentum and increased confidence. This allows you to take on bigger, more complex habit changes in the future.

Schedule Your New Habits

Sixty-seven percent of self-made millionaires in my study maintained a to-do list. To-do lists are a way of processing success into your life. One of the tricks self-made millionaires use is to incorporate certain good daily habits onto their to-do list. These specific daily habits show up automatically, every day, on their to-do lists. This forces accountability. Every day you must be accountable for the new daily habits you are trying to form. If they are simple daily habits, after a few weeks, you won't need to include them on your to-do list - they will have become habits. You can then move on to other, new daily habits using this to-do list habit process.

Firewall Your Bad Habits

One trick to habit change is to make it harder for you to engage in a bad habit by creating some type of firewall between you and the bad habit. For example, let's say you eat junk food late at night while watching T.V. You eat that junk food because it's in your pantry. If it wasn't in your pantry you wouldn't be able to eat it. The way to make this bad habit harder to engage in, would be to stop stocking your pantry with junk food and instead stock your pantry with healthy snacks. The habit isn't eating junk food; the habit is snacking while you watch T.V. Eliminating junk food may stop you from snacking, but more likely, when you sit to watch T.V., the cue, you will default into your routine of seeking a snack. This time, however, the reward will be a different snack, ideally a healthy one or at least a low-calorie substitute.

Another bad habit might be spending hours on Facebook at night, after dinner. One way to make this habit harder to engage in would be to turn off your computer, or moving your computer into the basement or disconnecting it from the router. Because it requires exerting some effort to engage in the bad habit, you won't, if your willpower is weak. And willpower is usually at its weakest at the end of the day.

PART V
CASE STUDIES
– RICH HABITS
AT WORK

DR. BEN CARSON – RICH HABIT: DAILY SELF-IMPROVEMENT - READING

Ben Carson is a world famous neurologist who was raised in one of Detroit's ghettos. His mom was afraid that her son would become just another casualty of ghetto life. To prevent this, Mrs. Carson made Dr. Carson read every day for self-education. To ensure her son did his daily reading, she also required that he write a one page summary about what he read each week so she could read it. Each day, Dr. Carson would go to the library and spend hours reading. At the end of the week he would hand a summary of what he read that week to his mom for her to review. This daily reading Rich Habit opened Dr. Carson's eyes. He read stories about the lives of other poor, self-made millionaires. He began to think that if they could rise from poverty to wealth, so could he. Eventually, this daily reading became a habit that helped inspire Dr. Carson to try harder in school. As his grades improved, he gained confidence. This confidence made him believe that he could go to college, then on to medical school to become a doctor. He continued to read and learn every day throughout his adult life. Eventually, he became one of the most famous and respected neurosurgeons in the world. What I find most interesting about this story is that many years after his mom forced this reading Rich Habit on him, Dr. Carson learned that his mom was illiterate. She never actually could read any of his weekly summaries. Intuitively, Mrs. Carson knew that if she could instill in her son the daily Rich Habit of reading it would help get him out of the ghetto and set him up for success in life. And it worked!

ARNOLD SCHWARZENEGGER – RICH HABIT: PURSUING YOUR DREAMS

Arnold Schwarzenegger first gained international celebrity as a professional body builder and then went on to become a Hollywood celebrity and politician. But it all started for Arnold when, as a teenager, he stumbled upon a magazine featuring Reg Park, the famous actor who played Hercules in a very popular Italian movie series that began back in 1961. Inspired by Park, Arnold began working out with weights and his dream of becoming the world's greatest bodybuilder was born. Arnold's single-minded focus on realizing his dream is legendary. Two months prior to a Mr. Olympia body-building contest, Arnold's father died. His mother pleaded with him to return to Austria to attend the funeral. Arnold said no. He told his mom it would distract him from his training. Years later, Arnold would confess that his decision, although the right one for him because he won the title, damaged his relationship with his mother and his girlfriend at the time. Neither could understand how his dream took precedence over the death of his father. But Arnold's dream did take precedence. It took precedence over every part of his life. Arnold picked up his first barbell in 1960. Ten years later he earned his first Mr. Olympia title. Ten years dedicated to pursuing one singular dream. Arnold would apply his laser-like focus in pursuing other dreams, such as becoming a famous actor and, much later in life, Governor of California. While Arnold is an extreme example of focus, his story does highlight the importance of a single-minded focus in pursuing your dreams.

RICHARD BRANSON – RICH HABIT: CREATING MULTIPLE STREAMS OF INCOME

Richard Branson is one of the most fascinating self-made millionaires of the 21st century. He puts the Rich Habit of having multiple streams of income on steroids. Branson does not rely any single source of income. He has hundreds. Branson started and grew 400 companies in a vast array of industries that includes: music retailer, music record label, music video producer, an international airline, a rugby team, spacecraft manufacturer, telecommunications, mobile phones, fitness centers, book retailer, book publisher, book distributor, alternative energy, banking, venture capital, travel agencies, hotels, ski lodge, spas, passenger bikes, racing team, radio, railway and many others. What makes Branson unique is that he has failed often, made thousands of mistakes and yet, despite those failures and mistakes, remains fearless and passionate about pursuing every challenge and every new opportunity. His desire to expand the Virgin brand is really a desire to expand his streams of income. Branson learned very early on that this Rich Habit creates the most wealth.

ROBIN SHARMA –
RICH HABIT:
GETTING UP EARLY

Robin Sharma is a world renown leadership expert, personal and professional development coach, consultant to fortune 500 companies, professional motivational speaker and bestselling author with over six million books sold. Sharma attributes much of his success to the Rich Habit of waking up early. He likes to call his early morning routine the "5 AM Club". This is the time of day Sharma gets in his exercise, reading, meditating and prep work for his day. This singular Rich Habit has created a wealth empire for Sharma that makes him one of the most famous leadership experts in the world.

JACK CANFIELD – RICH HABIT: FIND A MENTOR

Jack Canfield, author of the Chicken Soup of the Soul series and Success Principles, holds the Guinness World Record for most books sold by an author - 500 million. He is also considered the #1 Success Coach in America. His seminars, training programs and coaching programs teach tens of thousands his success principles each year. How did he do it? Canfield was mentored by C. Clement Stone, a legendary personal development expert who also mentored Og Mandino, a former publisher of SUCCESS Magazine and author of The Greatest Salesmen in the World, a book that sold over 20 million copies. But Clement was only one of Canfield's mentors in life. Others who helped mentor Canfield include: Mark Victor Hansen, Janet Switzer, John Gray, Bob Proctor, Jim Rohn and John Maxwell. That's a lot of mentors!

APPENIX
RICH HABITS
TRACKING
SCHEDULE

TRACKING SCHEDULE

		WEIGHT	RUN/ JOG ETC	SPORTS	B	L	D	T	CUM CAL	AVG CAL
BEG										
GOAL										
END										
GOAL	2000 CALORIES									
DATE										
SUNDAY	1/1									
MONDAY	½									
TUESDAY	1/3									
WEDNESDAY	1/4									
THURSDAY	1/5									
FRIDAY	1/6									
SATURDAY	1/7									
SUNDAY	1/8									
MONDAY	1/9									
TUESDAY	1/10									
WEDNESDAY	1/11									
THURSDAY	1/12									
FRIDAY	1/13									
SATURDAY	1/14									
SUNDAY	1/15									
MONDAY	1/16									
TUESDAY	1/17									
WEDNESDAY	1/18									
THURSDAY	1/19									
FRIDAY	1/20									
SATURDAY	1/21									
SUNDAY	1/22									
MONDAY	1/23									
TUESDAY	1/24									
WEDNESDAY	1/25									
THURSDAY	1/26									

FRIDAY	1/27								
SATURDAY	1/28								
SUNDAY	1/29								
MONDAY	1/30								
TUESDAY	1/31								

MONTH	RUN/ JOG DAYS	MIN	MILES	AVG CALORIES	LBS (LOST)/ GAIN	BEG WEIGHT	END WEIGHT
JANUARY							
FEBRUARY							
MARCH							
APRIL							
MAY							
JUNE							
JULY							
AUGUST							
SEPTEMBER							
OCTOBER							
NOVEMBER							
DECEMBER							

About the Author

Tom Corley understands the difference between being rich and poor: at age nine, his family went from being multi-millionaires to broke in just one night. For five years, Tom observed and documented the daily activities of 233 wealthy people and 128 people struggling with poverty. He discovered there is an immense difference between the habits of the wealthy, particularly self-made millionaires, and the poor. During his research he identified over 300 daily activities that separated the "haves" from the "have nots." The culmination of his research can be found in his #1 bestselling book, Rich Habits – The Daily Success Habits of Wealthy Individuals.

A dynamic and empowering speaker, Tom travels the world, motivating audiences at industry conferences, corporate events, universities, multi-level marketing groups and global sales organizations. He has spoken on the same stage with many famous entrepreneurs and personal development experts such as Richard Branson, Robin Sharma, Dr. Daniel Amen and many others.

Tom has shared his insights on various national and international network, cable and Internet television programs such as CBS Evening News, Yahoo Financially Fit, Money.com, India T.V., News.com Australia and a host of others. He has wowed listeners on many prestigious nationally syndicated radio shows including the Dave Ramsey Show, Marketplace Money and WABC.

Featured in numerous print magazines, such as Money Magazine, Inc. Magazine, SUCCESS Magazine, Entrepreneur Magazine, More Magazine and Kiplinger's Magazine, and various online publications including USA Today, CNN, MSN Money, SUCCESS.com, Inc.com and the Huffington Post. Tom is also a frequent contributor to Business Insider, Credit.com and has been profiled in SUCCESS Magazine.

National publicity has garnered international media attention for Tom and Rich Habits research. Broadcast media, online publications, and television throughout Asia, the South Pacific, Europe, the United Kingdom, and Central and South America have supported Tom's powerful message.

In an effort to help adults instill good habits in the younger generation, Tom released his second book, Rich Kids – How to Raise Our Children to be Happy and Successful in Life. Rich Kids was the self-help category winner of the 2015 NY Book Festival.

Tom is also a CPA, CFP and holds a Master's Degree in Taxation. As President of Cerefice and Company, CPAs, Tom heads one of the premier financial firms in New Jersey.